BEADS

OF THE WORLD

A Collector's Guide with price reference

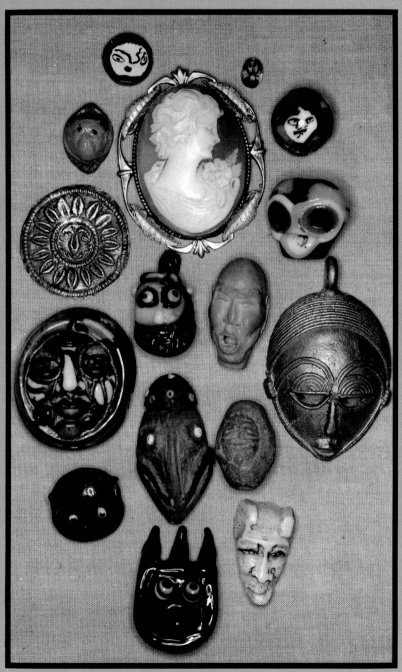

Peter Francis, Jr.

Schiffer Publishing Ltd

77 Lower Valley Road, Atglen, PA 19310

Dedication:

To Patti, Libby and Michael, who went before us and left trails of light.

ACKNOWLEDGMENTS

Hundreds, perhaps more than a thousand people and institutions, have helped me over the years to gather the information distilled in this book. They cannot all be listed here; they have been acknowledged elsewhere, and all are thanked again.

For this work, special thanks go to Nancy Schiffer, always helpful and enthusiastic as editor and to Mom and Dad, The Rev. Peter and Phyllis Francis. Mom put in many hours proofreading and Dad is the ever helpful "go-fer." Over the years no one person has been so generous to the Center in terms of both literature and examples of beads as Elizabeth Harris of Los Angeles, who deserves individual recognition.

The price guide was an particular task, and I am grateful to many who helped me with it. For carting me around, answering questions, letting me poke through their shops or other help, thanks to: Bead Werks of Los Angeles; Nikki Stessin of Beadworld of Seattle; Joyce and Jeff Griffiths of Byzantium of Columbus, OH; Kathryn Collins of Bead Needs of Portland, OR; Anita Malsin of Dáva of Portland, OR; Penny Diamanti of Washington; Steven and Duangporn Dunning of Hands of the Hills, Mercer Island, WA; Elaine Feldman of Los Angeles; Margaret Haldeman of San Francisco; Andy Hale of Anahita Gallery of Santa Monica CA; Valerie Hector of Chicago; Carol Hubbard and Pam Collins in Columbus, OH; Susan Mickiewicz of Ethnic Arts of Berkeley CA; Eric Gorbman of Monsoon of Seattle; Howard Newcomb and Alice Scherer of Portland, OR; Rita Okrent of Los Angeles; Naomi Rubin of Originals of Evanston IL; Albert and Ella Summerfield of Seattle; Dick Wezelman of Berkeley CA; Joyce Whitaker of Cambridge, MA; Marion and Murray Winagura of the Winagura Co. of Culver City, CA; Marilee Wood of San Francisco; and Toshiko Yoshida of Los Angeles.

For those that promptly sent catalogues, I thank Beadbox of Scottsdale, AZ; Beadazzled of Washington and Beadzip of Falls Church, VA; Beads Galore of Tempe, AZ; Bovis Bead Co. of Tombstone, AZ; Oriental Crest of Houston; Out on a Whim of Cotati, CA; Picard African Imports of Carmel, CA; Shipwreck Beads of Olympia, WA; and TierraCast Specialty Findings of Santa Rosa, CA.

Frontispiece

Faces in beads. Outside clockwise from upper left: polyform bead by Nan Roche, face mosaic by Brian Kerkvliet, north Indian glass face bead, Turkish face bead, Baoule brass mask pendant, Egyptian ivory bead, face bead by the Sacred Eye, Venetian face bead ca. 1950, porcelain mask pendant by Joyce Whitiker, silver sew-on ornament from Iran, monkey face bead of faience by Carol Strick. Inside clockwise from top: cameo pin/pendant ca. 1880, carved pit from China, stone bead from Afghanistan, mask carved from pit from Papua New Guinea, glass face-mask pendant by the author.

A popular glass bead world-wide is made with a translucent red (or other color) glass over an opaque white (or other color) coat, commonly called "white hearts." The six larger ones on the top are all wound, the nine smaller ones below are drawn. All probably Venetian.

Published by Schiffer Publishing, Ltd.
77 Lower Valley Road
Atglen, PA 19310
Please write for a free catalog.
This book may be purchased from the publisher.
Please include $2.95 postage.
Try your bookstore first.

We are interested in hearing from authors
with book ideas on related subjects.

CONTENTS

A selection of mosaic beads from Venice, commonly called "millefiori" or "a thousand flowers." These have been popular trade beads for the last century.

These strands of European trade beads, with an emphasis on red, end in a incised bone pendant. There are many stories about them, but they are worn as adornment by Ethiopian women.

45.00
65.00
strand

U.S.A.

Mexico

Mediterranean

Atlantic
Ocean

5
Peru

Brazil

Pacific
Ocean

Sketch map of the world showing places frequently mentioned in the text.

Large glass bead resembling a marble. Possibly German, late 19th-early 20th century.

40.

Key to the Map

Countries:
1. Afghanistan
2. Austria
3. Burma
4. Chad
5. Columbia
6. Czech Republic
7. Egypt
8. Ethiopia
9. Germany
10. Ghana
11. Ivory Coast
12. Korea
13. Mali
14. Mauritania

15. Nigeria
16. Pakistan
17. South Africa
18. Thailand
19. Uzbekistan

Islands, Towns, Etc.
20. Borneo, Indonesia
21. Cambay, India
22. Hebron, West Bank
23. Java, Indonesia
24. Purdalpur, India
25. Shandong Pen., China
26. Venice, Italy

Russia

France
9
26
Turkey
Iran
Egypt
22
14
13
7
4 Sudan
15
10
8
19
China
1
16 24
India
3
21
8
Japan
12
25
The
Philippines
Indonesia
23
20
Angola
17
Indian
Ocean

A fishbowl or aquarium bead by Brian Kerkvliet, a contemporary American glass bead craftsman. *Courtesy Brian Kerkvliet*

Two large powder-glass beads made by the Krobo of Ghana, West Africa. The yellow one is a traditional Adjagba bead. The blue one is newer.

A strand of Japanese beads from the Edo period (1615-1857). *Courtesy Albert Summerfield.*

PREFACE

Three large beads made by inflating a glass tube by hand. The beads are decorated with a lattice of colors. Collectors call them "lace beads," apparently Venetian, late 1800s.

THE ROOTS OF THIS BOOK

I came to beads through two curious routes. One was travel and the other collecting. These are usually contradictory. Collectors like to stay in one place and maintain their holdings. Wanderers do best when they travel light.

Beads have long called me. In the late 1960s when I wore them as an emblem of my generation, I remember staring for what seemed like hours at a medieval rosary bead intricately carved from box wood in the Cloisters Museum in New York. In the early 1970s when I lived in Morocco, the glass trade beads being sold to Americans and Europeans fascinated me. I bought a few and kept them in a small black box, which I would open occasionally to view my treasures.

Going across North Africa I spent other hours gazing at the amazing glass head pendants which had been excavated at Carthage in Tunisia. But it was when teaching in Iran that I decided to collect beads. While my colleagues were busy buying carpets, I was gathering these little jewels. Soon I realized that no one really knew much about them. Being on the road, I had the opportunity to find out. Hobby grew into avocation and then into full-time career.

I have always been a collector. When younger it was stamps and coins, rocks and shells. Later I graduated to less well documented things: pop music memorabilia, antique maps, playing cards and then beads.

Beads make a perfect collectible. Small and easily cared for, they offer plenty of inexpensive examples to get one started and enough rare ones to keep one interested. I was convinced of their potential and could foresee bead shops, bead collector's organizations, bead catalogs, bead conventions, bead auctions, specialized collections and all the trappings of a hobby like stamps.

Much of that has now come to pass. Shops selling beads can be found in every city of any size. Bead Societies are now all over the country and even abroad. There have been several bead conferences, and others are being planned. More has been published on beads in the last ten years than in the hundred years before.

Unfortunately, much information available to the established or potential bead collector is not really very good. It is not that it is inaccurate, though it often is, but that it only repeats old stories and dealer's accounts, and those tales didn't tell us much.

Researching beads is hard work. It involves trudging down dirty country roads, scaling steep hills, wading through rivers holding a camera bag above your head and seeing, eating and listening to strange things. It also includes days in dusty libraries, which may or may not yield anything of interest, and hours negotiating with border guards or museum officials.

Need I say that it is also incredibly rewarding? It has taken me around the world many times (eight at last count), taught me several languages and opened dialogue with a marvelous variety of people. And it's work that has to be done if we are ever going to learn the truth about beads. We don't have the whole story yet, but it is now falling into place. It's not really the tale of pretty little gew-gaws. It is the chronicle of our brothers and sisters around the world and throughout time.

INTRODUCTION

Hold it in your hand. Turn it around and look at it. Then look at it more closely. It's a wonderful little object. A miniature work of art. Someone applied a lot of skill to it, and long before it was formed other people gathered raw materials for it, worked out a technology to make it and prepared a distribution system for it. This little jewel has a lot to say, once we learn how to listen to it.

People come to beads through many avenues. Some just like the way they look. Others are most fond of wearing them. Still others derive pleasure from making them into necklaces, sewing them into beadwork or creating other forms of jewelry. There is a growing body of people whose primary pleasure in beads comes from collecting them. This does not exclude any of the other things people do with them, but the collecting of beads is relatively new.

What is it about beads that fascinate so many people? There is their intrinsic beauty. There is the thrill of being on the ground floor of a growing hobby, with all the potential advantages of price increases and maybe even profits. But there is more, much more.

A serious interest in beads views these considerations as secondary. The primary reason so many people have become involved with beads is that their story is the story of people. It is not simply the mechanics of collecting small perforated objects. Rather, a window to the world is opened to anyone passionate about beads.

Bead collecting is people oriented. This is so for several reasons. First of all, there would be no beads if there were no people. People make them. They buy, sell, barter or trade them. They use them. And in the end they dispose of them in one way or another.

Bead collecting is also very much a people's hobby because of the delightful people you meet who collect or deal in beads. Bead people are a very mixed lot. Some are travelers; others are artists. Some make beads; others study them. Some are interested in one part of the world; others are most devoted to certain bead materials. No one is excluded no matter how they come to beads.

An intriguing mix of people is sure to enter your life when you begin collecting beads. If you attend a bead society meeting you may be transported to the amber mines of the Dominican Republic, heirloom bead lovers in a village in the Philippines or an archaeological site in the Middle East. When you visit a bead shop you can smell clove beads from the Persian Gulf, marvel at the glass technology of romantic Venice and maybe even meet a bead runner who has just arrived from Gambia, West Africa.

If this sounds exciting and inviting to you; if these possibilities pique your interest — come aboard. Join the bead world. There's lots of room and lots of adventure, even if you don't travel beyond your own neighborhood.

Bead collecting is challenging. It is not as neatly laid out as the collecting of many other things. Your library has catalogs and other books which include all the stamps ever printed and coins minted. Most stamps and coins carry the names of the issuing authority and many of them are dated. With a little practice, you can look up any stamp or coin you have and know when and where it was made, in what quantity and for what purpose.

If you are more inclined toward natural history, stones, shells, fossils or even beetles may interest you. Here again, though not every specimen (certainly not every beetle) has been classified, it is not too difficult to figure out the basic story of most items in your collection.

People have made instant collectibles out of the stuff of their own nostalgia. Phonograph records and old cameras, dolls and political buttons, Valentine Day cards, salt and pepper shakers and beer cans all have their devotees and their own catalogs.

Chinese carved bone beads. Bone does not carve as well as ivory, but these are sold as replacements.

.50 per Bd

3 - Strand
5' -
Rare

Beads in the Pacific paradise of Hawaii include the polished, dark nut of the candlenut tree and white shells. The large shell lei was given to tourists. The valuable leis are made of small dove shells found on the beaches.

There is also a class of goods manufactured specifically for a collector's market. Plates, medals and coins, miniatures and small ceramic or glass sculptures fall into this category. Production is controlled by one or a few companies. You always know what you have and how many other people have them as well.

All of this fine. There is nothing wrong with any of these other hobbies. It is just that beads are unlike them. I know of only two or three that carry the legend "Made in...." You rarely see one with a date. There are no standard bead catalogs. People interested in beads must do some digging themselves to learn about them. A decade or so ago this was all but impossible for the average collector.

Why? Because beads come in an immense and bewildering variety. They have been around for some 40,000 years. There is probably not a country in the world that doesn't make beads of some kind, and this was as true in the past as it is now. Beads can be made from anything solid. Even with glass, the most important bead material, there are numerous ways to shape, color and work it.

So, bead collectors have to play detective. They have to train themselves to look for the subtle clues that help distinguish one bead from another. They have to learn to apply tests and examine beads with an experienced eye. They have to be ready to exercise their brains a little to figure out what a given bead's story may be.

Is this difficult? No, not really. It's fun. It's a task that was inconceivable until recently. We have learned so much about beads in the last twenty years or so that most of what was done before is now sorely outdated. We have also learned how to identify beads and how to put together all the little hints we gather to pinpoint the origin, date and use of a bead.

I can hear some of you asking this: "If beads have been around so long and are found everywhere, why didn't we know more about them earlier?" It's a question I've wondered myself for a long time. At first I assumed it was partly sexist blindness. In our modern society beads are usually "just women's trifles" and most academics, museum personnel, archaeologists, historians and anthropologists have been men.

But I think the reason goes beyond that and is linked to the limitless variety of beads. There are so many of them, made of so many materials, from so many places and times and used in so many ways that the task was daunting. It would take — it has taken — a few dedicated people to devote their whole lives to the subject. It is a topic that needs to be viewed universally, because the bead story is cut from whole cloth.

Few people were ever willing to try to do this. Those who began never finished. It was easier to rely on old myths about beads and pass on tales invented by dealers to make a sale than to discover the truth about them.

But the breakthrough has been made, and this book is an indication of that. We do not try to cover all beads nor all beadmaking industries here. We cannot be comprehensive in any one volume, no matter how large. What we can do, however, is introduce you to this fascinating hobby. By concentrating on the beads you are most likely to encounter in a collection, shop or elsewhere we hope to acquaint you with a booming and successful new hobby.

This book will be an eye-opener to some, who had no idea that the subject of beads was so large, so colorful and so stimulating. It will provide you with hints on how to get started collecting beads, what to do with them, and something about most of the beads you will meet. It is intended to be accurate, but not to furnish all the intricate details that are involved in many of these beads. For that purpose, notes and a reference section have been set aside in the back of the book for anyone who wishes to follow particular themes in more depth.

This book is designed to launch you as a bead collector or advance further a hobby already begun. As you read through it, remember that it only scratches the surface of a vast subject. But beads are always kind to people and everyone is invited to love them in whatever way suits them.

Welcome to the World of Beads!

CHAPTER ONE
THE UNIVERSAL APPEAL OF BEADS

The bead story has roots stretching back to the first modern humans. They are still very much with us. Their eternal appeal has never failed.

They are also universal. Beads are found everywhere. There are no people without them. There is probably no country in which they are not made. Some societies do not value them as highly as others, but periods of bead scarcity are usually followed by a profusion of beads. Nor are they an exclusively female adornment. In most times and places men wear them, too.

Beads have been part of the human condition so long that we overlook the contributions they have made. Those interested in fine or costume jewelry say they have no time for beads. But, beads are where it all began.

Beads are worn at bodily constrictions (head, neck, wrists and waist) or wherever they can dangle (hair, ears, even the nose). Beads were first worn at all these places. As metal became available, bands and then bejeweled creations replaced them. Necklaces became collars and torques, headbands became tiaras and crowns, bracelets became bangles and short strings of beads became earrings. Beads are the basis of all jewelry.

The one exception is the pin. Bone and metal pins were worn to keep garments closed. We still wear pins, though now as brooches and not to fasten clothes. Even if beads weren't the forerunner of pins and brooches, they commonly decorate them. A look at costume jewelry will show you that beads remain basic elements.

There are other silent contributions of beads. Much exploration, long distance travel and trade was for beads or bead materials. The bead trade is tens of thousands of years old. Many technological developments resulted from figuring out how to make a bead from a new material. To appreciate the complex story of beads and how they developed into the extraordinary variety that we see now, we shall glance at their past. If you think what happened long ago has no bearing on us today, think again. The bead story is timeless.

THE OLD STONE AGE

Our remote ancestors improved on their animal skills by turning stones into simple tools and building shelters from sticks, mud and grass. They tamed fire and explored and settled the globe. We don't know how they thought, but I imagine they appreciated a spectacular sunset or gorgeous flower, the song of a bird or whistle of the wind. They no doubt imitated some of nature's glory. They painted their bodies with colorful clays and told stories around the campfire. They sang and danced and made things just for the joy of it.

By the time modern humans emerged 40,000 or more years ago they had a concept of art for its own sake. The first evidence for this is in the beads, the oldest known art form. Beads precede cave paintings and carved figures. They are the earliest known expression of the creativity of the human soul.

The first beads were probably made from easily gathered attractive materials: seeds, berries, leaves, flowers and feathers. Unfortunately, our knowledge of them is hampered because they do not survive burial and we cannot examine them tens of thousands of years later. The earliest beads on record were more durable. Chief among them was shell: marine, fresh water and sometimes fossil. Bone was next favored, both massive mammal bones or thin, often hollow bird bones. Animals that supplied the bones were also eaten, which was not always the case with the shellfish. Teeth, including ivory, which had to be worked, is the other major material of Old Stone Age beads.

Beads are the basis of much jewelry. Beads in jewelry are fun to collect because pieces are sometimes marked with the place of origin, though this does not always guarantee the beads were made there. The pin at lower right is marked "France," but the beads are probably Czech or Austrian. However, the two lower left earrings are marked "Japan" and have typical Japanese beads.

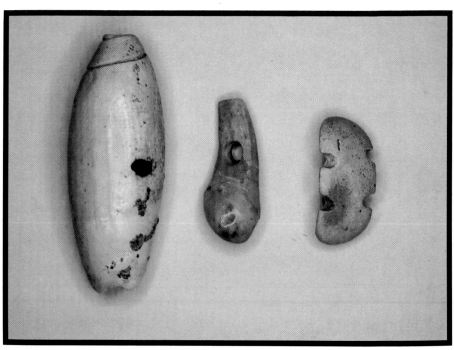

Some ancient beads from the second millennium B.C. The olive shell from India has been perforated on the top and the side. The red deer tooth and bone spacer are from Iran.

The pattern is the same wherever we look: Europe, Asia, Africa or Australia (we still lack data from the earliest inhabitants of America). The other major material not recorded in Europe or Australia is ostrich eggshell. Even though this was the "Stone Age," stone beads were quite rare; stones were tools to break, drill and grind the finished beads.

This may seem like a very remote time not relevant to a modern collector, but these materials continue to be used for beads and are most honored in some places. Shell remains a key bead material in our day. Ivory is still beloved. Seeds, bones, teeth and even ostrich eggshell beads are on the market, and some are the basis for spectacular collections.

Moreover, these materials are often worked in the same way and into the same forms that were popular long ago. To cite one example, 25,000 years ago on the lush prairies of central India lived a bird safe from most predators, even though ostriches cannot fly. Humans probably didn't kill many, because an ostrich can outrun a car and kick hard enough to kill a horse, but the clutches of eggs left unguarded when a curious bird investigates a strange noise is a feast. One egg is as large as 40 chicken eggs. An empty egg makes a perfect water container for people with no pots. When it breaks it can be made into beads. To do that, circlets were chipped from the shards, then drilled with a pointed stone. After many had been drilled they were put on a fiber or stick and ground along a stone to smooth them. This polished the edges and made the beads all the same size.

This is a clever way to make thin disc beads from flat materials. The idea spread and 10,000 years ago we find it in North Africa and China (where dinosaur eggs were sometimes substituted). The technique is now used all over the world. We call it the "heishi method" after the word for shell bead in the language of the Santo Domingo Pueblos of New Mexico. Handmade heishi is laborious and expensive. In the Philippines they turn it out mechanically by the ton, and the economy of Santo Domingo has suffered as a result.

So, the next time you have beads made this way (unless the strand is tapered, they will all be the same diameter) you have a lot to consider. The ancient method spread to all corners of the globe long ago. It recalls the connection between ostriches and humans. And the bird, which we now think of exclusively as African, has become extinct in many places, an early victim of human exploitation, including the by-product of beads.

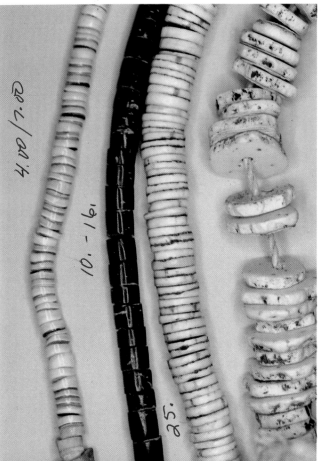

The heishi technique is widely used to make disc beads. The left strand is marine shell from the Bahamas. The second strand is dark coconut shalll from Africa. The third strand is ostrich eggshell from southern Africa. The right strand is ostrich egg chipped and prforated but not yet ground down into discs.

THE NEW STONE AGE

Archaeologists call the changes during the New Stone Age a revolution. Indeed, it was. People began to settle in agreeable places, plant grains and domesticate cattle. They built villages and improved their tools by grinding them to a point instead of just chipping them. They invented pottery and the potter's wheel, the bow and arrow and fire-machines.

And it was a revolution for beads as well. The security of people with an assured food supply allowed more time and effort to be spent on beautifying themselves. Trade increased and more exotic shells, stones and other objects were introduced. Inventiveness came to the fore. Metals were discovered: copper, lead and gold were easily spotted and made into beads. All metals known to the ancient world were first used for beads (except for tin, whose first use was as a bangle). The same was true later with glass, and more recently for plastic and aluminum.

People wanted more colorful and harder stone beads. The technique for grinding tools was applied to beads (or the other way around). But the most difficult problem was perforating the bead. The earliest methods included gouging with a sharp rock, scratching repeatedly in one spot, sawing with a stone blade and widening natural holes so a string would fit through. However, harder stones require a more sophisticated approach, and thus was born the drill. A stone-tipped stick or a stick with an abrasive like sand could drill into softer stone by being twirled between the palms of the hands. The holes were large and hour-glass in profile and the opening or aperture was eccentric or off-center.

However, with a string wrapped around the drill and attached to a bow, the driller could control his movements better and speed up the work. This bow-drill (and the pump drill in some places) was a advanced tool. It is an early application of rotary motion. We don't know if the bow-drill developed from the bow and arrow or vice-versa. Bow-drills are still used to make beads. The largest stone bead industry in the world, in western India, continues this time-honored method.

CIVILIZATIONS TO EMPIRES

Villages grew into towns and then cities. City-states were born and "civilization" took on meaning: writing and warfare, temples and taxes, kings and priests. Wealth was concentrated in sanctuaries and palaces and a class of artisans grew up to serve their patrons. The desire for ever more luxurious goods resulted in long-distance trade networks for such scarce bead commodities as carnelian, amber, pearls and lapis lazuli.

Bronze and iron were no longer luxuries but the stuff of common tools. From the techniques of building hot furnaces came new materials of elegance: faience and glass. Faience is similar to glass, but the particles of sand do not completely fuse, only melting on their surfaces to join. Over this core is a glaze, a thin layer of true glass. Faience beads enjoyed 2000 years of popularity before they were replaced by glass.

Stones drilled before the introduction of diamond tipped drills. Notice the hourglass shaped holes, made with a stick and abrasive or a stone drill. These tab pendants from the America southwest are Mogollon or Anasazi, ca. A.D. 900-1400.

Faience, like glass, is made from quartz, but the particles of the core do not melt. The glaze, a true glass, is only on the surface. On ancient pieces the glaze has usually fallen off. Top left: New Kingdom Egypt crumb bead. Two middle top: Roman period pendants. Top right: New Kingdom pendant representing the god Bes. The other beads are from Iran and Afghanistan, ca. 1000 B.C., though the ducks (or hens) might be older.

An early application of glass was to glaze stones. These quartz beads were glazed to make them shiny and gave them a blue coating, now mostly gone. Persian, possibly 2nd - 6th century A.D.

Stone beads were extremely popular, and techniques were developed to improve on the basic stone. The first use of glass was to put a thin glaze on some stones. Certain stones could be colored, and others were decorated with patterns. All these innovations lead to a greater demand for beads.

Although some of the earliest kingdoms were fairly extensive, they could not compete in size with the later development of Empires, which ruled over many different people. Persia, Rome, China and India developed into empires as one dynasty gained domination over all its neighbors. Each of the great empires was wealthy, with strong upper and middle classes who wanted ever more symbols of opulence. Trade between them accelerated and much of the trade was in small luxuries like beads.

BEADMAKING AND BEAD TRADING NETWORKS

This very brief recounting of the growth in beadmaking and use should help us appreciate the great chronological depth that many modern beads and processes have. It is also designed to give us some background when we consider the levels of bead networks.

A bead network consists of at least a beadmaker and a customer. In the earliest periods, there was not much more. Someone would find a suitable material, say a shell, and bore and string it. The ultimate customer might be a sweetheart, a child or someone willing to exchange a basket of berries for it. The system is simple, and the distance involved measured in one or a few hundred miles.

Such small scale bead networks survive to our day, though jet planes and the tourist industry now spread beads much farther than before. From the shell workers of Kanniyakumari, India to the amber workers in Simojovel, Mexico, beadmakers participate in industries that have primarily local impact.

The next stage in the growth of a bead network is a regional system. These commonly concentrate on products which are relatively scarce. They trade over thousands of miles and involve many different people. Often a raw material is found in one place, refined in another and finished into beads in a third, near the customers.

One example of regional trading networks is the old lapis lazuli trade. The precious blue stone is only found in quantity in northern Afghanistan. From there it was shipped to a city several hundred miles south, where the less valuable calcite matrix was removed and top grade material was shipped hundreds of miles west. At the second city beads were made, and these were then shipped more hundreds of miles to the ultimate customers in the great cities of Mesopotamia (modern Iraq) and Egypt.

The western Indian agate and carnelian bead industry is very old. The long thin bicone is a type exported to Sumeria (modern Iraq) as early as 2000 B.C. The agate beads are called "babaghoria" after the patron saint of the industry. The flat round beads were made from plugs taken from finger ring production. The large flat bead in the center was popular in Afghanistan, while the diamond shaped beads were enjoyed by Romans.

Carnelian was involved in a similar pattern. The stones are found along the Narmada River in western India. They were refined and made into red beads in the great cities of the Indus Valley Civilization. While some were worn locally, others were shipped from the Arabian Sea up the Persian Gulf to the Kingdom of Sargon the Great.

Yet another instance happened in the New World. The wealthy were able to afford importing raw materials and finished beads over great distances from all directions. The fabulous contents of Tomb No. 7 at Monte Albán, Mexico, demonstrate that. It has a wealth of jade from Guatemala or Costa Rica, amber from southern Mexico, pearls and thorny oyster shells (Spondylus) from the Pacific or Gulf of Mexico, turquoise from northern Mexico or the American southwest and gold from many quarters.

It was only when kingdoms grew into empires and began trading with each other on a scale that was then global (they didn't know about America) that bead networks became world-wide in scope. Such large networks cover tens of thousands of miles. They include multiple centers of sources and of beadmaking, and their products become basic trade items. Throughout history, there have been six such truly global networks. Their beads dominate most collections, and all of them continue to operate to this day, though some are stronger than others. The six are:

1. *The stone bead industry of western India.* The main products are red carnelian and brown onyx, though other stones are cut there now as well. It is some 4000 or 5000 years old, and has provided the bulk of carnelians to the world market since time immemorial.

2. *The coral bead industry of the Mediterranean.* Precious red coral grows best in the Mediterranean Sea, and it has been a favored bead material for thousands of years. It is fished on both the northern and southern coasts, with European production going to Europe and later its colonies, the Egyptian harvest going to India and the northwest African yield going to West Africa. For 2000 years India has been the greatest single customer of precious coral.

3. *The eastern Mediterranean glass bead industry.* This is where glass began, and glass beads from various centers in the Near East have supplied an ever-increasing market. By Roman times these beads were going to every corner of the known world. In the Islamic period, production continued and the beads were traded in even greater quantities and varieties. The European Crusaders and Asian Mongols devastated the Middle Eastern glass centers, and the industry only lives on at a few small centers.

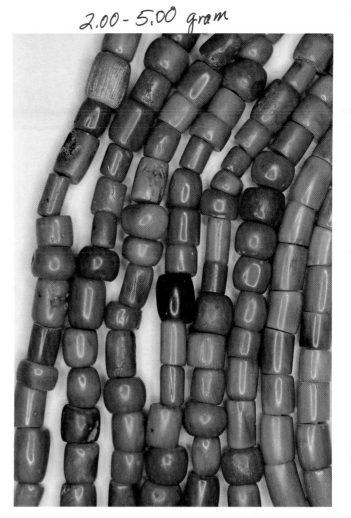

Precious red coral lives most successfully in the Mediterranean Sea. A desired gem for thousands of years, it has been fished and worked at many places along the coast, to be sold to the world.

Glass beads of the Eastern Mediterranean lands are often spectacular and complex. It can be difficult to separate production of Roman, Byzantine and Early Islamic times. Counterclockwise from left around the lamp: torus folded bead (probably Early Islamic), combed wave bead (ca. 4th century B.C.), mottled crumb bead. On spout of lamp: green mosaic bead (ca. first century A.D.), yellow date bead. Clockwise from top within the lamp: green and yellow date beads, triple silver-glass bead (Egyptian), mosaic eye bead (Early Islamic), agate-glass pendant (ca. first century A.D.), simple wave bead (perhaps Syrian), brown and white agate glass bead (Early Islamic).

Small drawn, monochrome beads are found for nearly 2000 years throughout the Old World. Called Indo-Pacific beads because of their distribution, they were made in southern India and in ancient cities now located in five other Asian nations.

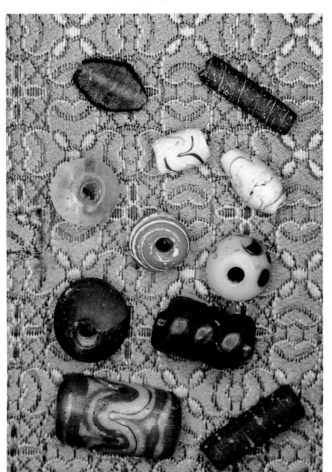

4. *The Indo-Pacific bead industry.* These beads are small and come in a limited range of colors, yet for 2000 years they were the greatest trade bead, indeed, the greatest trade item of all time. The beads were first made in southern India several centuries B.C. They are still made there, but in the first century or so beadmakers moved to now long forgotten cities in Sri Lanka (Ceylon), Vietnam and Thailand. Around the seventh century the Srivijaya Kingdom based in Indonesia and Malaysia took over the Southeast Asian branch and new centers flourished for several centuries. Only a remnant survives now in a small village in southern India.

5. *The Chinese glass bead industry.* Not much was known of this industry until recently. The Chinese do not wear many glass beads themselves. But their export drive and greater foreign exposure begun a thousand years ago saw Chinese beads flood the markets of neighboring Southeast Asia and reach as far west as East Africa. After the discovery of America, they poured into Mexico and California with the Spanish via the Philippines and into Alaska with the Russians via Siberia.

6. *The West European glass bead industry.* This is the newest of the great bead industries. Though glass beads were made in Europe for a long time, the export network was only developed around A.D. 1500 when Europeans began to explore the globe. Venetian, Dutch and Czech beads were given away, bartered and sold to people who mostly ended up as colonial subjects to Europe. This industry remains very strong and its products are among the most varied and commonly collected today.

Summary

Few private collections are going to have many beads that are thousands of years old. Surprisingly, however, such old beads can be found and many collectors will have some. But even if you have no ancient beads, understanding the history of beadmaking leads to a greater appreciation of all beads in your collection.

Many beads easily available today were made by the same methods employed ages ago. And every bead made today has a story behind it, sometimes reaching back tens of thousands of years. This is part of the joy of bead collecting. It puts you in touch with the whole world, not just geographically but through time as well.

The Chinese have only recently been recognized as major glass bead makers and traders. These beads are from archaeological sites or are heirloom beads in the Phillippines, Borneo and Thailand. They all date to about the 14th or 15th century.

During the last 500 years western European glass beads became the most common and widespread trade beads in the world. At top are small drawn striped beads, Venetian. In the center are amber colored and red glass bead necklaces from Bohemia. The bottom is a strand of blue beads decorated with goldstone from Venice. Late 19th to early 20th centuries.

15. - 30. Sf.

3.00 - Sf

14

Collecting is a very personal activity. There are as many different sorts of collections as there are collectors. Everyone has a different idea about what to collect and what to leave out of a collection. Decisions are made on the basis of your interests, the time and space you have and your pocketbook. No one can tell you how to form a bead collection, but there are some hints that can get you started or improve a collection already begun.

WHAT TO COLLECT

An initial decision will be what to collect. Major collections usually have a mixture of single beads and bead strands, along with other bead collectibles.

Collecting individual beads has several advantages, cost and storage among them. Many people form type collections and strive to obtain examples of every type of bead or of every type of certain kinds of beads. It is common for these collectors to keep two or three of each bead: two if they ever want to make a necklace from them; the third one reserved for trading with someone else. Complete strands come the way of these collectors, too, who may elect to break them up and trade the rest or keep them intact.

Others maintain that the minimum unit of beads is the strand, and they acquire complete necklaces or strings of beads. Some are inclined to keep the necklaces together just as they get them, others form strands (24 to 30 inches — 60 to 75 cm — long) of only a single type of bead. Strands are certainly impressive, but it should be remembered that by the time a strand of beads reaches you it may not be composed the way it was when it was originally worn. Many dealers mix miscellaneous beads together or match beads of one type, and beads pass through many hands before they come to you.

My advice is that if you receive a strand that is strung up in the way it was worn, it should be kept together. If you are going to break it up, you might want to take a picture of it to keep a record of how it was used. If beads are simply strung up by dealers, there is no reason to keep them together. Such strands are often a jumble of beads not very artistically arranged. Dealers' strands from West Africa are most often strung on the leaves of the raffia palm, a tough grass-like fiber.

Typical shapes of beads. Top row from left: sphere, the more common oblate with flattened ends, annular or ring and disc. Second row: cylinder, square cylinder and hexagonal cylinder (the cross section is named first if it is anything other than round). Third row: barrel, hexagonal barrel, ellipsoid (without flattened ends). Fourth row: bicone (two cones joined at the bases), square bicone, truncated hexagonal bicone. Fifth row: rectangular tabular (perforated through the edge), diamond tabular, cornerless cube (cube with corners removed), melon (grooves running from end to end).

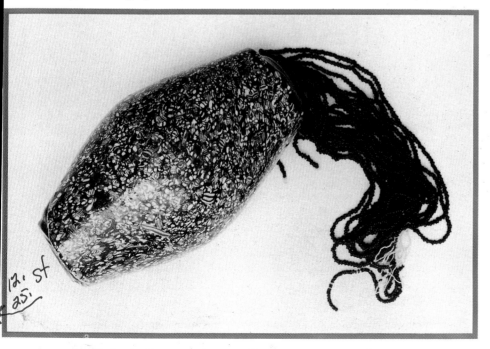

Strands and single beads. The largest and smallest glass beads currently made. Two dozen strands of the smallest drawn beads from southern India fit into the perforation of the largest wound bead made in northern India.

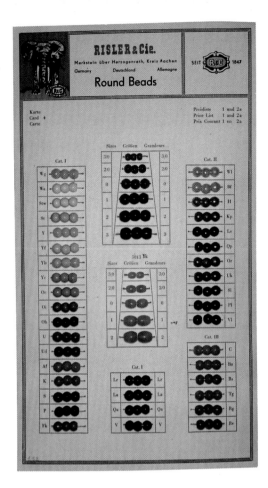

Sample card of Risler and Co., near Aachen, Germany. Glass beads were made by the Prosser technique, then tumbled to remove the mold seams. Production of beads at this company ceased in 1957. Cards like these are invaluable in helping us piece together the history of beads.

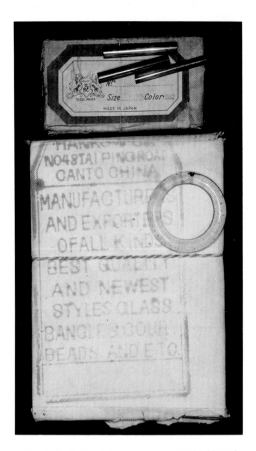

Beads in their original packages are highly collectible. The white box contains yellow rings made in Canton (marked "Canto") China. The brown box on its end has long drawn blue beads made either in China or Japan (marked "Made in Japan"). Both are from the early 20th century.

Another sample card, this one from Czechoslovakia from the turn of the century. The beads closely resemble contemporary Venetian foil and other lamp-wound beads.

75.00

A beaded leather cigarette or tobacco case from England. One side has "E. Shields" spelled out in cut steel beads. This side reads "July 12 1846."

Card 75.00

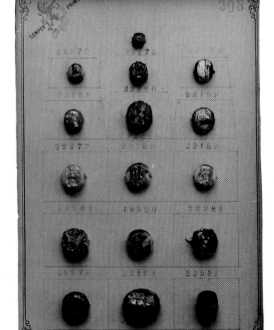

Another decision to make is what groups of beads to collect. Some people want the world and will try to form a bead collection that reflects a global perspective. Do you want every sort of bead ever made or do you want to specialize? To specialize you would concentrate on one class of beads. This might be determined by material (beads of shell, glass trade beads, stone beads), location (beads from Africa, India or Venice) or specialized use (beadwork, rosaries, amulets and talismans).

There are other ways to collect beads involving imagination or focusing on specific interests. Beadwork (items decorated with beads) can form a huge collection by itself. Bead sample cards, used by manufacturers to send to agents who sell beads, are highly collectible, though often hard to find. Beads in their original packages are very interesting. Those more academically inclined may work toward a large bead library. There is also a large and growing segment of "beadana," collectibles which celebrate beads in different ways, ranging from old cigarette cards to bags, pins and posters issued for bead conventions.

An advantage of collecting beads is that they can be used. Bead collectors have a handy selection of accessories for any occasion. Some people wear their favorite strands and place them back into the collection when they are done. Others like to make strands or other forms of jewelry with beads they have collected. They may make a new necklace for a special occasion and disassemble it later. Still others find intense pleasure in designing necklaces or other beaded objects, and these become the focal point of their own collection.

An even bigger step is taken by a few collectors, for whom the hobby develops into a career. Many, probably most, bead dealers began as collectors. Collectors often augment their income (and help pay for their collections) by making necklaces or earrings from beads they are willing to sell. Good bead stringers and beadwork repairers are always in demand. Some collectors are even crazy enough to become full-time bead researchers.

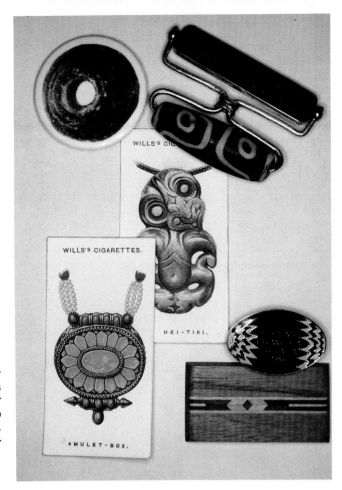

A selection of beadana made to commemorate or celebrate beads. At top left is a pin for entrance into the bazaar at the Bead Trade in the Americas conference, Santa Fe, 1992. Top right is the identification pin of the Second International Bead Conference, Washington, 1990; the glass bead made in India resembles a dZi bead. The cards are "Lucky Charms" cigarette cards issued by Wills in England in 1923. The pin on the bottom is the identification for the First International Bead Conference, Long Beach, 1985; it rests on the top of the wooden box in which speaker's pins were presented.

Beadana includes an increasing number of paper items. The poster was made for the Turkish tourist office in the 1970s. At top left is stationary made by Jane Olson. The card at an angle is made by Lois Rose Rose. The post cards are, from top down, by Beadazzled of Washington, DC; the Bead Museum of Prescott, AZ; Byzantium of Columbus, OH; and the Second International Bead Conference in Washington, DC.

A rainbow wall of beads. Many dealers and collectors enjoy arranging their stands in colorful spectra such as this one in a dealer's home in Los Angeles. *Courtesy Rita Okrent.*

STORING BEADS

Storing beads will depend on what type you collect. You will probably begin with every type of box and bottle you can get your hands on, but as your collection grows you will want to be more systematic.

Strands can be hung effectively; at least one collector decorates her bathroom with them. If you can't put nails or hooks into your wall, pegboards, cork tiles or acoustical tiles used for ceilings will work. You may arrange your strands any way you wish; a color spectrum can be beautiful. Each strand should carry a little tag saying where you got it, how much you paid for it and what identification you have for it. If you have many strands of one kind or want to rotate the collection, excess strings can be stored in cartons.

Single beads need to be separated into small groups. Commercial plastic boxes work, though they are not cheap. Many people are happy with baby food bottles (the top of a bottle can be nailed to the underside of the shelf above to give you two rows per shelf). I find a good system to be the plastic storage drawers set into metal frames sold principally for work-shops. Each drawer can contain one type of bead or be subdivided to hold several types. Be sure to label each group of beads. Larger drawers, such as the thread cabinets I bought from a notions shop going out of business, can be subdivided with a variety of small boxes, even match boxes.

For temporary storage or sorting, the plastic containers from super-markets can be used. I like the clear square ones we buy mushrooms in. One large collector uses egg cartons for permanent storage. He cuts the top and bottom apart and uses the bottom for single beads and the tops for strands; they are all kept in cardboard cartons. If you can get your hands on a map case or similar file with large, thin drawers, these can work quite well.

Fortunately, most beads do not need much care. They were made to be durable to begin with. Of course, you do not want to drop or chip or crack them. The more delicate the material (amber, jet, pearls, horn and ivory for example), the more care is needed for them. One word of warning: shells (and pearls) should not be stored in wood, cotton or paper (unless acid-free). Wood products emit a gas which eats at the shell. Plastic and metal containers are preferred.

FINDING BEADS

Where do you go to find beads? The answer is: everywhere. Across the U.S. and increasingly elsewhere, specialized bead shops are flourishing. Most can be found by looking under "beads" in a telephone directory. If you are going to buy by mail, the names of many dealers are found in the ads in *Ornament* magazine and in *The Bead Directory*. There are a growing number of bead societies around the country, and most hold bead sales bazaars once or twice a year. Bead conferences, such as the biannual Bead Expo, attract a hundred or more dealers. For addresses of these organizations, see the Appendix.

There are many other sources as well. Antique shops, or any antique or collectibles show will have some beads. So do flea markets, rummage sales and even yard sales. Many people inherit beads from an older relative. These can be a great windfall, but don't fall prey to the "grandmother syndrome" and assume that just because she was 90 when she died the beads must be that old, too. Keep your eyes open; you will be surprised at where you can get beads.

Travel is an excellent opportunity to buy beads. The beads sold in other parts of the world may be quite different from what you get at home. Find out as much about them as you can, and remember to bargain hard where it is required. Bead Tours also exist (see the Appendix).

No matter how isolated you may be geographically, beads are not far away. Join one or more of the bead societies, even just to get their newsletters, and begin corresponding with members who share your particular interests. Beads can be swapped just as easily as any other collectible.

How much should you pay for a bead? This book is designed to help answer that question with the price guide. It should be obvious by now that we cannot picture and price every bead on the market, but we have chosen a selection that reflects major market segments.

As with all collectibles, the principle ingredients in the price are the quality and condition of the piece and market forces, that is supply and demand. Quality is very important with certain beads, especially those of natural materials. With some stones, for example lapis lazuli, the top quality may be found in only two percent of available material, which itself represents only the top 30% of raw material. How well it is cut is also a factor in price. Condition is often more of a consideration than scarcity unless a given bead is very rare.

Two types of beads call for special consideration because their collecting is a matter of ethics as well as taste. Both are available in the market, but any large-scale collecting of them will lead to cultural or ecological destruction.

One are ancient beads. Most ancient beads have only one source: archaeological sites. Peasants are hired by agents of international dealers to dig where an ancient city was once located. Whatever is found — ceramics, bronzes, gold or beads — is then sold for a handsome profit. This illegal excavation, best known as "looting," completely destroys the information that would be gained about the past if the site were scientifically excavated. Archaeologists are not looking for treasure. They are after answers about how our ancestors lived and how we came to be what we are. They should be respected. Buying looted beads is destructive to the world's cultural heritage.

The other are beads made from endangered species. Everyone is aware of the international outcry against the poaching and needless slaughter of elephants for their tusks. But, many other endangered species are still being made into beads: "tortoise shell," many corals, some shells and the teeth and skin of several animals. Old beads, imported into the country long ago, made of these materials are legal to own. New ones should be avoided.

Storing single beads or even strands is easy in drawers a few inches deep and small enough to be removed. They may be subdivided by all sorts of containers. This is the Center for Bead Research's primary drawer of the Chinese bead collection.

HOW BEAD RESOURCES DEVELOPED

As with any collectible, there must be a foundation of information available to the would-be collector. Depending upon the character of the collectible, that information is more or less easy to find. With the enormous variety of beads, the task has been difficult. Because of the nature of beads, most research on them has been done by archaeologists, with anthropologists and historians helping out.

The first people who studied beads were more-or-less enlightened savants who collected old things and tried to learn about them during the early 1800s. There was no scientific archaeology or similar discipline applied to their queries. These precursors of archaeologists are referred to as "antiquarians." Some were reasonable, others were crackpots. Since little was really known about beads, almost anything could be said about them. The late 1800s raged with a debate about the origin of Venetian chevron beads. One writer thought his was brought to England on the neck of a Nubian slave of a Roman soldier, while another claimed that their discovery in American Indian graves proved that the Phoenicians sailed to the New World.

As archaeology grew up, so did bead studies. Early in this century there were a few papers written with a more scientific outlook. The man who came to dominate the field, however, was not a trained scholar. Horace C. Beck was one of Europe's finest lens grinders, but retired from the family firm after contracting the great "Spanish" flu of 1918. He devoted himself to his hobby, and the leading archaeologists of the time (many being fellow Englishmen) flocked to his simple country house to seek his opinion. Beck never discussed the social aspect of beads, but his reports on beads from around the world remain masterful descriptions.

Beck died in 1941, when the globe was already plunged into the chaos of World War II. Following that conflict came the Cold War and decolonization. There was no one to replace Beck, and bead research fragmented, with people interested only in the beads of their country, and hardly ever communicating with any others. Only two people, the Dutchman W.G.N. van der Sleen and the Englishman Alastair Lamb, tried to take a global view of beads. Both, however, were handicapped by working largely in a vacuum.

A change began in the late 1960s and early 1970s when beads were part of the costume of many young Americans, and a demand for interesting beads opened a flood of imports from West Africa. Some people began collecting or at least accumulating these beads, and even opened bead shops. The fad died out by the late 1970s, but by that time three institutions had been set up to pay serious attention to beads. The *Bead Journal* (now *Ornament*) was begun by Robert Liu in 1974. In the next year he and some other bead lovers began the Bead Society in Los Angeles. Lapis Route Books, devoted to publishing the facts about beads, was founded in 1979.

The *Bead Journal* grew slowly. A few other Bead Societies were begun, but times were rough for a few years. But in the early 1980s a combination of events began to put bead studies on a firmer foundation. The Rochester Museum and Science Center held the first conference on glass trade beads in 1982 (and one on shell beads in 1986). The Bead Study Trust was set up in England in 1981 and the Society of Bead Researchers in the U.S./Canada in 1982, both appealing mostly to professionals. The Center for Bead Research acquired permanent quarters in Lake Placid, N.Y. and the Bead Museum was opened in Prescott, AZ in 1985. At the end of 1985 the Bead Society (Los Angeles) celebrated a decade of growth with the First International Bead Conference on the ship *Queen Mary* in Long Beach, CA.

The field has boomed since then. Collectors are no longer forced to rely on erroneous second hand information and specious stories about the ages and origins of beads. Many of the most vexing problems about them have now been solved, and there is a great deal of support, both personal and in written form, for anyone seriously interested in beads. While the resources in the Appendix didn't even exist a few years ago, the list will be incomplete as soon as this book has gone to press. Bead collecting is growing that fast.

Beads strung on wires and made into flowers were used for mourning in France, but mostly for decoration in the United States.

This does not mean we know everything about beads. There is much yet to learn and every bead collector has an opportunity to add to our knowledge. If you have discovered a new bead or bead industry or something interesting about beads that no one knew before, you can be part of the exciting detective work now going on. There are many outlets for you to make your discovery known. Depending upon your inclination, you can inform one of the existing institutions, you can give a talk to your local bead society or write in one of their newsletters or any of the other publications that feature beads. Any such activity will bring satisfaction, because you will be part of a world-wide effort to learn more about beads.

And why bother about beads at all? Not for their own sake, though they are fascinating — even, some say, addicting — in their own right; but because the story of beads is the story of all of us.

Even the literature of beads is becoming collectible. The July 1971 edition of *Arizona Highways* ran a long feature on trade beads. The first edition of *The Bead Journal* (forerunner to *Ornament*) and of Joan Erikson's *The Universal Bead* are also collector's items.

CHAPTER THREE
THE USES OF BEADS

Children learn to use and string beads early. The larger package was for children to string beads on pins as "friendship pins," a craze in 1983. The smaller package is of Japanese beads sold to Korean children.

In the 1960s the craft of knotting thick cords, called macramé, was popular. Beads with large holes were made especially for the craft. The two finished weavings are from India.

What are beads for? The most common answer is that they are strung into necklaces or made into some other ornament. In a sense this is true. Decorating the human body has always been their most important use. However, this is only part of the story.

Beads serve us in many ways which differ from culture to culture. They are interesting in their own right because they tell us about how other people think and act. Understanding the various ways of employing beads helps us to identify where and by whom they were used. There are also some small perforated objects often mistaken for beads; some people collect these along with beads.

Certain instances of how beads are used may strike you as strange or far removed from our lives. For some people the whole point of collecting is getting to know other people in other places through one of their most intimate and personal belongings.

But we must keep in mind that our world of supermarkets and fax machines is just as exotic to other people as grass huts and food served on banana leaves is to us. Nor have we left beads behind in our modern world. Look around: they surround us. A cross, a star of David or a Mercedes Benz hood ornament strung on a chain immediately tell you something about the person wearing them. So does a full set of perfectly matched natural pearls. No one is surprised to see a beaded curtain or a beaded mat on a driver's seat; they are some of the practical uses of beads.

SPECIAL DECORATIVE BEADS

The primary purpose of beads is to be decorative. Many people put them on their animals and more recently their cars and trucks, in their homes or on any number of other objects. Beaded curtains, beaded lamp shades, beaded dresses and beaded bags are just a few of the ways beads enliven the artifacts of our lives. Most of these beads are almost universal and can fit into any decorative scheme, but others are made for particular purposes. Beads made for specific uses are common in any collection, and their names and functions should be understood.

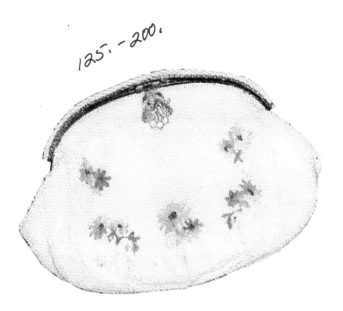

125. - 200.

100. - 150

In addition to being used for beadwork, small drawn "seed beads" can also be used as elements in necklaces. This beaded collar comes from Canton, China, ca. 1985.

Two beaded purses of the 1920s or so. The right one has an Art Deco design and contains many brass beads along with black glass beads. The left purse is typical of French production of that time, with embroidered flowers on a white beaded background.

Pendants hang down from a strand. From the top left is Chinese glass imitating carnelian, a blue penguin from India and a Czech "lightbulb" pendant. Middle row is Peruvian clay, shell leaf from Veracruz, Mexico and an onyx pendant from Egypt. Bottom row is a "propeller" pendant from Korea and a molded glass "jade" imitation from Japan.

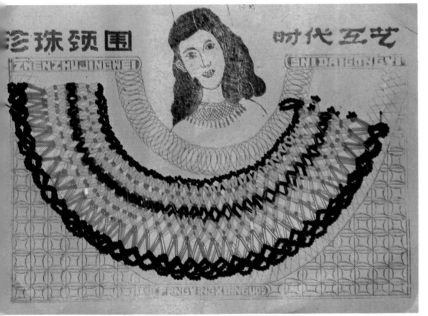

2.00 - 4.00

.90 - 3.50

.80

.25

1.00 - 1.50

2.50 5.00

"Seed bead" is the name popularly given to small beads used in beadwork. The term is a little confusing, since many seeds are used for beads, but it is well established. The best seed beads are uniform in shape and color, but many pieces of beadwork may have older beads. Seed beads can, of course, be strung by themselves without being used for beadwork.

Beadwork refers to objects decorated with beads, especially seed beads. The subject of beadwork is large and has a specialized literature all its own. People of many different cultures have done and do beadwork, and there are many variations among them. Beads may be sewn onto cloth, paper or leather; woven into a net or lattice that stands by itself or decorates the surface of something; or woven into cloth on a loom. Many different stitches are used to apply beads. For more detailed information, see some of the books in the Appendix.

Pendants are beads which hang down from a strand. They are often the centerpiece of a necklace or the highlight of a piece. They may be suspended by a loop or a hole off-set from the center of the bead.

Spacers have multiple holes to keep two or more strands apart. The two on the left are Czech glass. The diamond shaped carnelian one is from India. The round green one is Indian glass. The large square one is bone painted with an old Persian scene. The white one on the bottom was made by Joyce Whitaker of the United States.

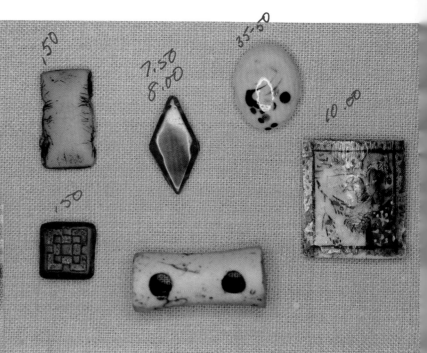

Spacers are beads with two or more perforations that allow several strings to pass through them in separate paths. Most often, the holes are parallel and the spacer separates two or more strands of beads. Holes sometimes converge or cross to make other special effects.

Interlocking beads are made so that one bead will fit into its neighbor in order to make a smooth or tightly linked strand. While interlocking beads in ancient times were laboriously made individually from different materials, they are far more common in our day, made by molding, especially by the Prosser technique (see Chapter Six).

Toggles are long beads which project above the string as much as they hang down from it. Some common shapes include dumbbells (which can interlock) and those that look like rice grains.

Beads which interlock with each other is an old idea, but not widespread until efficient molds, especially the Prosser technique, were developed. Interlocking beads may be chevron shaped (called "snake beads"), have balls that interlock or be spool shaped. Most of these beads are probably Czech.

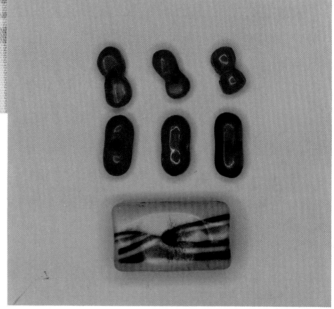

Toggles sit above and below a strand equally; they often interlock. The pink ones are coral. The red ones are Czech glass imitating coral, called "corales" in Mexico. The yellow one is also Czech.

BEADS AND MAGIC

Some of the most important and perhaps oldest uses of beads are for magic, superstition and religion. One can imagine a Stone Age hunter presenting a string of deer teeth to his mate with the implicit promise that he will always bring food to the campfire. On the other hand, the hunter may wear the teeth and claws of a bear or wild cat or dog in order to impart the animal's strength and cunning to himself.

The idea that a part of something or an object resembling something else can influence the course of events is deeply ingrained in many societies. Many beads are or were used with this concept in mind. Red carnelian was worn because it was the color of blood and therefore it was believed that it would stop the flow of blood. Milky white stones were worn by women who were hoping to increase their lactation and the health of their babies. Practitioners of many religions put bits of relics, some sacred clay, a prayer, a magic square or such items into a leather or metal case to keep the power of their belief with them always.

The most widespread example of beads in magic is connected to the superstition of the Evil Eye, common in much of the world. This notion holds that certain people (we might call them witches) have the power to bring misfortune to other people, cattle or even a house by using their Eye. In order to be effective, the Eye must strike the victim's eye at first glance.

This belief probably originated among herders in the Middle East during the New Stone Age. From there it spread throughout the Muslim world and around the Mediterranean. Still later, Spaniards, Greeks and Italians took it to America.

Naturally, one wants to avoid dangerous contact with the Eye. How can this be done? There are two precautions to take: you can be defensive and attract the Eye away or you can be offensive and attack it.

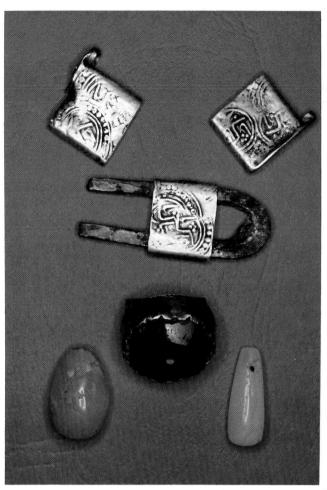

Materials function as amulets for several purposes. The silver case from Iran opens to reveal a piece of iron, which drives away the Jinn, a race of non-humans described in the Qoran. The carnelian bead has been mounted in silver to be worn to prevent blood flowing from a wound. White agate beads are used to increase lactation in Spain and elsewhere.

Cases which hold charms, relics or other items of devotion are common to several religions. Top row from left:Moroccan of leather, Moroccan of silverish metal. Second row: Indian of copper, silverish metal reliquary of a French saint. The bottom two stone beads cut as charm cases are from India; notice how the agate one (left) was cut to show lines at right angles to each other.

The Evil Eye is one of the most widespread of superstitions. The three top left beads are ancient stone and glass from the Middle East. The seven beads to the right are Venetian glass. The small blue bead in upper center is from India. The three beads at lower left are from Turkey.

The defensive strategy consists of distracting the Eye by making it look at something other than your eye first. What would divert its stare? Since the Evil Eye is looking for eyes, give it some harmless eyes to see. Representatives of eyes, whether dots, circles, circle/dots or more complex motifs are commonly used for this. Put on round beads, they make wonderful substitutes for real eyes, and a whole class of "eye beads" is thus born. Natural eye shapes such as cowrie shells and certain seeds perform the same task. All are most easily worn as beads, and all can be considered eye beads.

Other items will attract the Eye, too. The color blue is widely used in the Middle East, including blue beads for cattle. Silver is said to work, but not gold. Certain stones, especially agate, onyx and carnelian, are believed to attract the Eye. Once you begin to look, you will find there are many variations on this theme.

The other way to save yourself from the baleful influence of the Evil Eye is to attack it boldly. What more simple way to attack both eyes than by poking them out with two outstretched fingers? The hand is the most convenient and effective offensive weapon against the Eye. From this observation, hand pendants of all sorts came into use. In the Middle East they are mostly open palmed. In Europe the *ficus* or *higa* (thumb protruding from the first two fingers) is more common. Stars, crescents, doubled squares, the *corno* (a twisted piece of coral) and even chili peppers are all believed to work. So does a phallus and, by extension (I understand), a fish.

The hand, or a substitute, can poke out the Evil Eye. The silver pendants at top left and fish at bottom left are from Iran. The blue glass hand is Czech glass. The chili peppers are plastic from Mexico. The twisted red *corno* is from Egypt. The glass fish is from Turkey. The round red bead with stars and crescent is Czech; the heart with star mosaic chips is Indian.

An important counting function of beads is for prayers. The original prayer strand was Hindu, like the light wooden one made of Tulsi or Holy Basil from India. The black wooden strand is Buddhist from China. Both have 108 beads.

THE USE OF BEADS IN COUNTING

The nature of beads on a string all in a row enables them to be manipulated or checked off quite easily. This quality has given rise to different devices which are meant to help one remember something or to calculate arithmetic.

The earliest of these devices are prayer strands, designed to help the faithful keep track of their prayers or other devotions. Many of the world's religions use them. Within each faith there are often variations, but most are so distinct they can be identified rather easily. Prayer strands usually have a number of "small" beads, often equally divided by larger or different colored beads. There is commonly a tassel, large bead or some pendant at the end.

The first prayer strand probably was Hindu, as they are mentioned as early as 800 B.C. Hindu strands contain 108 beads (or a simple fraction of that number). Hinduism consists of several sects, the most important of which concentrate their worship on Siva or Vishnu. Those who worship Siva have a prayer strand (or sometimes a single bead) of the hard dark brown rough nut called *Rudraksha* (Shiva's eye). Those who follow Vishnu use the small light wooden beads made from *Tulsi* (holy basil).

Buddhism, which developed from Hinduism, took over the Hindu prayer strand and elaborated the function of each bead. The simplest Buddhist strands have 108 beads divided into four groups of 27. A more complex type developed in Tibet; small pendant strands were added for counting off the times and the decades of times one said one's prayers. A single strand like this was able to count off 10,800 prayers in one cycle.

From the East, the prayer strand traveled West to the Muslim world. There the strands are generally of 99 beads divided into thirds. These represent the 99 attributes of Allah, sometimes called "names," found in the holy book of Islam, the Qoran. It is said that Allah actually has 100 names, but the 100th one is known only to camels. One recites the names of God on each bead, "The Compassionate," "The Merciful," "The Beloved," and so on.

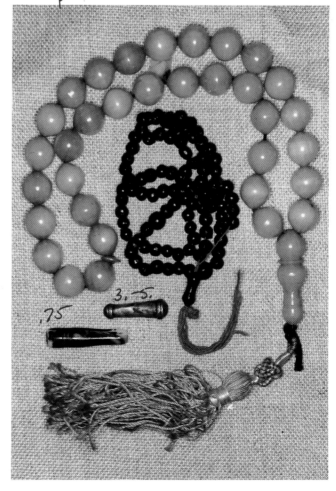

Muslim prayer strands usually have 99 beads, as does the black clay strand in the Center from Iran, or 33, as does the amber plastic strand from Egypt. The long counter, or Imam bead, is distinctive even when detached from a strand. The brown and white glass counter is Czech, the silver counter is Iranian.

Superficially resembling prayer strands, these do not have the proper number of beads to fulfill that function. Instead, men in many Middle Eastern countries play with them as "worry beads." These are both plastic; the white one bought in Greece and the black one in Lebanon.

There are <u>Muslim prayer strands with only 33 beads</u> and also some with <u>999 beads</u> (again only camels know the 1000th name). However, smaller strands with 12 to 20 beads on them which are seen in the hands of Turks, Syrians, Iranians, Lebanese, Greeks and people of some other nationalities are not properly prayer strands but serve only to give idle fingers something to do; the are usually called "worry beads."

The Roman Catholic rosary was likely borrowed from the Muslims during the Crusades, though St. Dominic is said to have introduced it. The "full Dominican" rosary consists of 150 small *ave maria* beads divided into fifteen groups of ten by larger *paternoster* beads. The "lesser Dominican" rosary, which is far more common, has only a third of these beads. There is a great variety of Catholic rosaries, devised for particular devotions by special groups. These seem to be most common outside Europe in countries such as India and the Philippines. A bead collection could consist entirely of different types of prayer strands.

Beads are efficient at counting not only prayers, but most anything at all. The most common device for general counting is the abacus. The early history of the abacus is obscure. It is first fully described only in the 1400s in China, though it may have existed much longer than that. Someone who knows how to use an abacus can count very quickly and accurately, easily beating adding machine operators in races, and still faster than most people who figure on a calculator.

The Chinese seem to have had the first abacus. It has a series of parallel wires, held in a rectangular frame with a horizontal bar in the center to divide the wires. Under the bar are five beads (units) and above are two beads (each equivalent to 5 units). Beads are moved to the center to register the numbers. The Japanese abacus dates from the 1700s or so, and while it is similar to the Chinese, there is only one bead above the bar. The abacus also also went west to Russia, Turkey and Iran, where it has no dividing bar, but ten beads, with the fifth and sixth differently colored; in these, the beads are moved to the left.

Some Christian groups have embraced the prayer strand, probably introduced during the Crusades. The typical Roman Catholic rosary is the Lesser Dominican with five groups of ten small beads separated by large beads. The outer strand shown here is made by knotting, and was used by monks in the all-male, 1000 year old theocracy of Mount Athos, attached to Greece.

Beads can be used to count anything. Putting them in a frame and moving them around can help an operator calculate very fast. This is the Chinese form of an abacus.

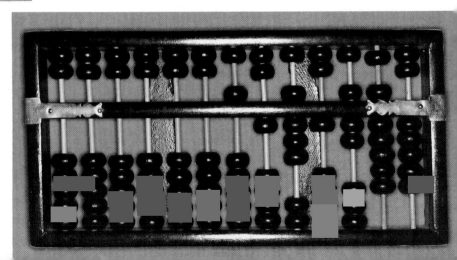

BEADS USED FOR MESSAGES AND MNEMONIC DEVICES

Beads can be used to send messages or encode them for later interpretations. Among the Zulu of South Africa, colors and patterns of beads have special significance. One of the most interesting items made with beads is called a "love letter." Girls get together with their friends and weave small rectangles of beads on a necklace. The colors and patterns signify everything from gossip to romance, and even a couple breaking up. These "love letters" are given to the boys, who never part with them, but keep them as a record of their affairs (they can even be introduced as evidence in court under certain circumstances).

In America, the most widespread use of messages in beads was with wampum. We often think of wampum as "Indian money," but it most emphatically was not. Wampum was sacred to northeastern Indians before the Europeans arrived. It consisted of small tubular beads laboriously cut and drilled from hard shells. When Europeans introduced metal drills, its production was sped up and enlarged. Since the mother countries did not want to lose coins in the colonies, Europeans (not the Native Americans) adapted wampum as currency; it was legal tender in all thirteen original states up to the mid-18th century.

Rectangular pendant woven from small glass "seed" beads by young Zulu women in South Africa. The colors and patters convey messages, most often about romance. This example may have been made for export.

A reconstructed wampum belt in the Six Nations Indian Museum in Onchiota, NY. The belt is called the Hiawatha Belt, symbolizing the unity of the original five nations which formed the Iroquois League. *Courtesy: Ray Faddon*

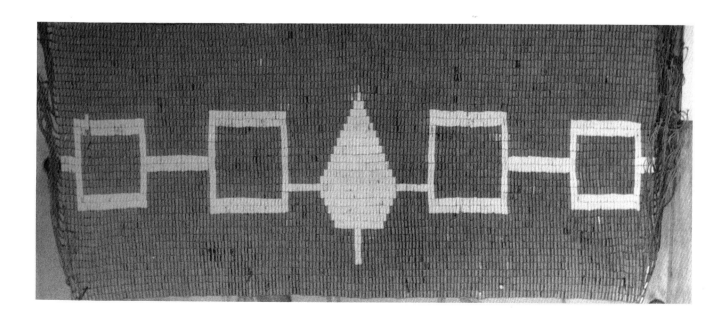

Among Native Americans, especially of the Iroquois League, wampum was employed at every significant turn of life. Red painted wampum was sent to other villages to indicate war. Short strings were used to call a council together. Councils could not meet without the proper seating arrangement embedded in a wampum string. Adoptions, deposing a chief, mourning, speaking at council meetings, treaties and contracts all called for wampum. Details of treaties were woven into wampum belts, which contrasted the more common white shell beads with the scarcer purple (also called blue or black) ones, obtained from the quahog clam. An expert could take a belt and read off the particulars of a treaty or other historical event by looking at the patterns and recalling the provisions or other nuances.

The importance of wampum was never lost by the Iroquois, though by the beginning of this century most of their precious belts were in White Men's museums. During the last few years there have been intense negotiations over these beads between the Iroquois nation on one hand and the governments of Canada and New York State on the other.

BEADS AS STATUS AND SOCIAL SYMBOLS

It doesn't take much to realize that someone with valuable beads is likely to be wealthy and even powerful. After all, diamonds, pearls and gold represent such things in our society. Many people use beads not only to indicate their wealth, but also many degrees of their social status.

Since beads can be symbols of wealth, and since a string of beads can be easily divided, it is not unnatural for them to serve as currencies or semi-currencies in different contexts. However, just because a bead is accepted in a barter does not make it equivalent to money, and their role as currency may have been overstated. But, they can and do serve as standards of value and units of wealth, are often acceptable against debts and sometimes act just like money.

In many cultures, certain beads are often reserved for people of particular rank. Bodom beads are the privilege of kings and other great men among the Asante in West Africa; Akosu beads fulfill the same role among the neighboring Ewe. In South Africa the Venda reserve the "beads of the water" for their elite, while Mutiraja beads are only for the princely families of some islands in Indonesia. These and other special beads will be discussed in more detail in the appropriate chapters.

On an even broader level, beads and other adornments (including clothes) identify the ethnic group to which a person belongs. In remote regions, such as rural mountainous sections of the world, people wear beads and ornaments which distinguish them from their neighbors. When you can read the language, the beads will immediately tell you to which village or ethnic or linguistic group a person belongs.

Depending upon the society, beads may indicate a person's position in life. Some show that a person is very young or has gone through a ceremony marking the beginning of life. Others distinguish a married from a single man or woman. Among the Zulu, girls who have been in love wear beads that differ from those who have not had any romantic attachments. Beads show which men are headhunters in some places, and they often indicate divorce or widowhood.

In India a woman is not given a ring upon marriage, but a strand of beads. North Indians wear the *mangalsutra*, with small black beads and some gold ornaments. The arrangements of these necklaces differ from area to area and community to community. South Indian Tamil women wear the *tali*, a saffron dyed string with a set of gold beads. Examine some of these beads more closely and you can even tell if the woman is a devotee of Siva or Vishnu. After her husband has died, a woman is expected to remove or even destroy all her jewelry.

Heirloom beads become particular marks of status in many cultures. They are kept either by everyone or only by certain leading families. The rules for their inheritance are different among various groups. The beads that are honored by one group are often of no interest to their neighbors.

50.-75.

Beads can be a store of wealth. This is obvious with precious metals, such as silver, and even more so when money is made into beads and pendants; all from Iran. Glass, stone and other beads may serve the same purposes.

By gram

Indian brides are not given rings but beads. The strands are Mangalsutras worn in the north (here plastic and glass have replaced gold). The black beads on them are called *potti*, a word recorded in the 12th century. The single, gold-washed beads are for a Tali for south Indian women; the name is recorded in the early centuries A.D. They would be strung on a saffron-dyed cord. The large pendants reveal religious associations; the one at bottom right is for a follower of Siva, the other for a Visnu worshiper.

During the Manchu dynasty (1644-1911) all court officials, military officers and their families were required to wear beads based on the Tibetan Buddhist rosary. Most such "court chains" were broken up after the Revolution overthrew the foreign dynasty. *Courtesy: Rita Okrent*

In some cultures, there have been laws passed requiring the wearing of certain clothes and ornaments by particular people. China is perhaps best known for this, and it was especially striking during the last imperial dynasty, the Qing (1644-1911). One mark of status adapted required officials, army officers, their wives and children to wear strings of "court beads," which were modeled on the Tibetan rosary. The Emperor himself had to wear prescribed ones to perform various duties. Other officials had some liberty in choosing the materials and colors of their beads, but of course were forbidden to wear those reserved for the "Son of Heaven."

BEADS AS TOOLS AND TOOLS AS BEADS

Beads have several characteristics that enable them to perform useful tasks. Their weight and the holes through them have been exploited by many people to hold down cloth or paper. The Chinese have used beads as weights on bed curtains and scrolls. Europeans use them for weighing down tablecloths, while Anglo-Indians found them handy for the edges of doilies put on the top of glasses or pitchers to prevent bugs from swimming in their drinks.

In India doilies are used to cover pitchers and glasses so that bugs do not fall in. They are weighed down by beads, these made in Purdalpur.

English lace makers attached a spangle to the ends of their bobbins on which beads were strung. These beaded spangles had several advantages. The different beads helped the women separate one bobbin from another and also prevented the round wooden bobbins from rolling away. Some pottery makers in India use a string of beads (both glass and stone ones have been recorded) to burnish the surface of their ceramics.

Yet, not all small objects with holes are beads; some were made for entirely different purposes. One will run across them when hunting for beads. It is best to know what they are.

The most common of these are spindle (or spinning) whorls, small weights made to go on a stick to give it momentum when spinning fibers into thread. Spindle whorls come in a variety of shapes, but they are as radially symmetrical as can be made, usually have large holes, and are often non-symmetrical in profile.

Also, one finds net weights used to hold down fishing nets and pendant-like loom weights used in weaving. There are pendant shaped black stones which may be worn, but whose function is to judge the purity of gold (or bronze in ancient times) as touchstones. There are also seals, many of them designed to be strung through a hole, that performed numerous services for ancient owners as signature, letterheads, notary seals and padlock.

Are these objects beads? The answer depends on how you define beads. My definition is functional: If they act like beads, they are beads. In this way a host of small objects from keys and safety pins to bullet cases and strips of plastic drinking cups are beads when they have been used that way. Seals have long been regarded as a subclass of beads, but no one I know wears fishing net weights. Spindle whorls are sometimes used as beads: I know of two archaeological examples (from Egypt and the Philippines) and one living one (from Iran), not to mention modern collectors wearing them.

The bottom line is: enjoy what you like. String them up to your taste. Like beauty, the definition of a bead is in the eye of the beholder. If we get too restrictive in our definitions, then abacus beads or beads in a rosary might not qualify. It is better to keep an open house than a closed mind.

Beads on "spangles" at the ends of lace bobbins in England prevent the bobbins from rolling around and aid in identifying the correct thread. English tinkers made beads for this purpose; these are typical of the Midlands.

Although often collected and strung as beads, these were originally tools, spindle whorls to help spin thread. Top row left is a glass one from the Roman period. Next is a small clay one from Iran and two clay ones from Columbia. Bottom row left is a clay one from India, a bone one from Iran and a black clay one from Mali.

SECTION TWO
BEAD MATERIALS

Japanese ojime. Center one is glass. Clockwise from top: ivory, coral, glass, lacquer, enamel and lacquer. *Courtesy Albert Summerfield.*

CHAPTER FOUR
ORGANIC BEADS

A multisectioned articulated fish carved from bone. This symbol of prosperity and good luck may also have religious significance, as it is used by Armenian Christians in Iran.

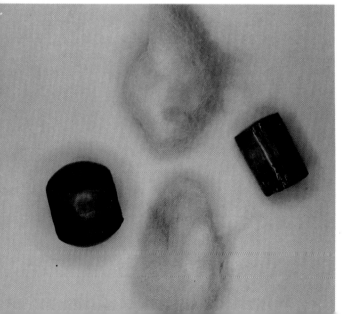

A drop of acetone paint thinner or nail polish remover will help show you if a bead has been dyed. Here a red wooden and a blue coral bead show traces of their dye on pieces of cotton.

As shown in Chapter One, the first beads were made of seeds and berries, bone and shell, tooth and eggshell. One of the marvelous qualities of beads is that they never really go out of fashion. Someone, somewhere is wearing beads today much like those worn tens of thousands of years ago. Before you label beads "primitive," think of some of our bead materials: precious coral and valuable pearls are products of sea animals; jet and amber are fossilized tree parts. Many less valuable beads made from plants and animals are also available to us. Some are home-made and others imported from around the globe.

Collectors can appreciate these beads on several levels. They are often quite beautiful. Others carry intriguing stories linked with their origin and use. Recognizing them can help identify the source of a particular strand. Still others are very expensive and go well with the finest jewelry anywhere.

There is such a variety of beads of organic materials that this chapter is devoted to the more important ones, and for convenience they are arranged alphabetically. Plastics are included in this group because, though many plastics are synthetic, the raw materials are organic.

With a minimum of equipment, you can fairly accurately learn to identify basic organic substances. If your interest is in categories with a large number of species, such as shell, wood and seeds, you will find it enjoyable to consult specialized books to make more accurate classifications of beads in your collection.

Two simple tests can be used. One is the "teeth knock" test, which simply consists of striking the object against your teeth. This will give an indication of how dense the material is, and can immediately separate certain classes (plastics from glass or stone, for example). The other is the "hot point" test for which you need a point that will heat up on one end while you hold the other end in your hand, such as an ice pick or long thin knitting needle. You heat the pointed end - even a candle flame does well - keeping the point away from the wax. Then lightly jab the tip in an inconspicuous place on the bead, such as in or next to the perforation. Cup your hand and smell the fumes, if any. This provides useful information for a number of materials.

The most important over-all tests involve your eyes and your brains. Nothing is more valuable than looking closely and intelligently at beads. I advise everyone to use a small hand lens whenever you go bead hunting and don't leave your thinking cap at home. I was once taken to the house of a wealthy woman to look at a necklace of large oval beads she had bought at an auction. She was disappointed when I told her they were plastic, and chagrined when I gently noted that a "tortoise shell" (for this is what she thought they were) is too thin a material to make such thick beads. Nothing beats a good look and some common sense.

Another test also comes in handy. Many natural materials are dyed. To see if a bead is dyed, take a drop of fingernail polish remover or paint thinner (they must be the acetone type) onto a piece of cotton or clean rag and rub the bead vigorously. Virtually any dye will be removed this way, as acetone is a nearly universal solvent.

Amber

Amber is the fossilized resin of trees buried some tens of millions of years. Sometimes insects or larger animals caught in the resin are preserved as fossils in this wondrous gem. Amber has been a favorite bead material since long before anyone can remember, and remains high on most bead lovers' lists today.

Imitations of amber abound. Glass used to be employed, but it is easy to spot; it is colder in the hand and harder when knocked against the teeth. But plastics are something else. Plastics are synthetic resins and most attributes of amber can be imitated in plastics. As a result, synthetic "amber" is the biggest rip-off in the bead world. I get knots in my stomach whenever I see a string of beads marked "amber" or "copal" with a fancy price tag when I know it is all plastic. Nor is it the uneducated who make this mistake; many people who should know better err as well. It is true that some old plastic beads are now very expensive in Africa, but they still should not be labeled "amber."

So, what do you do? Many people know that rubbing true amber against natural fabrics will charge it with electricity (*electron* was the Greek name for amber) and then it will pick up scraps of paper or hair. But, plastics made with a temporary anti-static agent (the agent is required so it will go through the molding or extruding machine) will act the same way.

Many people also know that rubbing true amber against the palm of your hand will yield a pine-like smell. Pine oil in the plastic can duplicate that. You see insects in the piece? Have you never seen a watch embedded in plastic? Amber is denser than most plastics. A solution of four table-spoons of salt dissolved in eight ounces of hot water will float amber, but it will also float some plastics.

The simplest test for true amber is this: jab the bead (near or in the perforation) with a pin. Natural resins chip. Plastics do not. If (when) a dealer objects to this test, check the beads carefully; many old beads will have already been chipped especially on the ends. Or promise that if it does chip, you will buy it.

Similar identifying problems occur with copal, a material much like amber but not as old and only semi-fossilized. Copal is not very common and you will not lose money if you buy copal instead of amber. The problem is that most material called "copal" is just plain plastic. Copal tests like amber, chipping with the jab of a pin, but will not build up a static electric charge.

2.00 – 8.00 gram

Amber's soft glow and other properties has made it a precious commodity for thousands of years. The ends of the beads on the strand are pitted because each was cut from a small nodule, saving as much of the material as possible. The top inside bead is ambroid, made by fusing chips of amber under pressure. Below it are two faceted amber beads, popular in the 1920s. Below them are two old wedge shaped amber beads from Iran.

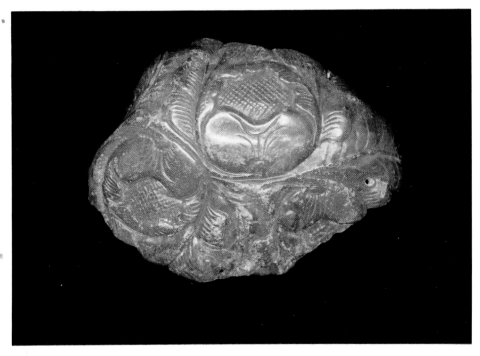

25.00

Related to amber is the semifossilized, younger copal. It has all the features of amber, but will not build up a static charge. This carved piece is Chinese, ca. 1900.

12.-15.

Bone is readily accessible and has been used for beads since the beginning. The two largest beads are bleached cattle bone from Kenya. The strand with skulls was carved in Nepal. The two beads in the center are from Iran, while the two rough ones at bottom left are deer bone from India.

2.-4. cm

There are many types of coral, some highly valued and others of lesser rank. The strand and four beads on the left are dyed corals from the Philippines. In the center are three small golden coral beads from Hawaii. Below is a black coral bead from Veracruz, Mexico; both types are "horny corals." At upper right is precious coral from the Mediterranean.

Bone

Fresh bone is dull white, has no reaction to the hot point test and will not scratch glass. It is one of several materials you need to look at carefully to determine what it is. Bones have tiny pores (blood vessels) or short grooves running their length, which result in a dotted pattern on the end of a bead. Bone is most often used as a substitute for ivory.

Copal — see Amber

Coral

There are hundreds of kinds of corals. The most important one is precious red coral (*Corallium rubrum*), which lives in the Mediterranean Sea and other waters with similar ecologies. Coral is actually the support structure built by innumerable small marine creatures.

Coral is widely imitated by many materials, especially glass and plastics. It is much softer than glass (glass scratches it easily) and harder than plastics in the teeth-knock test. Coral has no reaction to the hot point test. Many lesser corals are dyed darker red; try the acetone test to determine if a dye was used.

The easiest test for coral involves a close look. As precious coral grows, thin striations form on the supporting structure. These striations are parallel, but when they come to a branch of the coral they diverge to allow the branch to grow out. The cross section of a branch or a stem has distinctive concentric growth layers with fine radiating lines. This structure cannot be duplicated in glass or plastic.

In addition to precious red coral which is lime based, black and golden horn corals are also very popular. They, too, will have concentric growth lines, but not the striations along the side. The sources for many of these corals are becoming exhausted.

Flower Petals and Scented Beads

The petals of flowers may seem a strange bead material, but they are used especially by women and girls at home to make strands. There are a number of recipes for making them, but they all involve drying the petals, working them into a paste and forming them into beads. Usually, essence of rose or other scent is added to enhance the smell.

In the 1910s some companies sold "California Flower Beads" through mail order catalogues. They were advertised as being made from crushed flowers, but it now appears that most were actually dyed and scented plaster.

35. +

In the 1910s and 1920s, the Restall Bead Co. in Long Beach, California, and the Mission Bead Company in Los Angeles (they may have been related) made "California Flower Beads." These come in a variety of molded shapes, colors and scents. It seems that they used materials other than pure flower petals in their beads.

Scented beads of many kinds are enjoyed around the world. Sandalwood has been prized in Asia for centuries. Arab brides wear cloves. In Africa and Arabia beads made from scented resins are popular. One type is composed of several materials, including aloes wood, cloves, musk, ambergris, flower petals and aromatic leaves. These are mixed into a paste and beads are either molded or formed by hand. Another scented resin commonly called myrrh, though it is not the true or valuable resin, is shaped into beads, colored and given various forms in Western Africa.

Distinguishing all of these scented materials is difficult, though the scent may give a hint. None but the "myhrr" react to the hot point test, but all scratch easily. Homemade flower petal beads are usually less compacted than the paste beads from Africa or the Restall and Mission beads, and will easily flake away with a pin.

Horn — see Keratin

Ivory and Teeth

The teeth of animals, both carnivores and herbivores, are among the most ancient beads and pendants in the world. They are still used, and some of them, such as bore tusks, are highly prized. Identifying teeth by species can be tricky for lay people, but a zoo or university biologist might help.

Ivory is the teeth of large mammals, most particularly the elephant. It is a warm and handsome material, and the combination of enamel and gelatin in it makes ivory a fine medium for carving.

Unfortunately, the high price of ivory has made the poaching of elephants so profitable that there is a real danger to the survival of these magnificent and sensitive animals. There is now a virtual world-wide ban on the sale of new ivory, and it should be respected. It is not illegal, however, to buy old or fossilized ivory.

Elephant ivory is most easily distinguished by looking at a bead closely. The ivory has grown with tiny diamond shaped pores which contain a gelatinous substance that makes the whole piece so nice to carve. These

10.-15.   20. +

Scented beads are highly appreciated by different people. At top is a strand of sandalwood, cut in Bali. In the center is a Persian Gulf Arab bride's necklace of cloves and Venetian glass beads. The two beads on the bottom are made of a special scented paste, which contains several ingredients, including ambergris, from Tunisia.

3.00 per gram

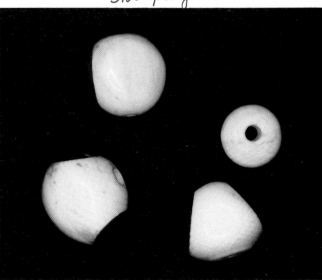

True ivory comes from elephant tusks. Its unique crisscrossed pattern is called Lines of Retzius.

Teeth are among the oldest recorded bead materials. This boar's tusk mounted onto a wooden figure of the rice deity is from the Bontoc of northern Luzon, the Philippines.

pores are arranged lengthwise along the tusk, but form a complex pattern of intersecting arches on cross section. These lines of Retzius have never been artificially duplicated, though some plastics replicate the outer striations.

The other ivory most commonly seen is walrus ivory. The walrus tusk is oval in shape and in the center there is an area that looks as though it had been crackled and glued together again.

Fossil ivory, mostly from Siberia, has become more important recently; it shows the lines of Retzius, but is duller in color than fresher ivory.

Increasingly popular as a substitute for real ivory is so-called vegetable ivory from the hard, dense nuts of certain palm trees. Different palms produce vegetable ivories. In India and Africa *Caryota spp.* nuts are used and in Latin America *Phytelephas macrocarpa*. The African variety is often called Doum and the American variety Tagua. Both carve well, are strong and solid and make good alternates to the animal products.

Vegetable ivory is made from nuts of various palm trees. On the left is a carved Doum nut from Africa. On the right is a Tagua nut from Central or South America.

Jet

Jet is a form of fossil wood. Its popularity for beads goes back to the earliest days, and important jet sources such as in England, Spain and Turkey have been exploited for many centuries. The heyday of jet in English-speaking nations was during Victorian times, when the popular English queen mourned her dear Albert for decades. "French jet" is actually black glass. Plastics also imitate jet.

Jet is actually a form of hard or vitreous-like coal, and shares the characteristics of coal. It is soft enough to scratch with the edge of a penny. If it is rubbed against the unglazed bottom of a plate or mug it will leave a brown (not black) streak. In the hot point test it will smell like burning coal.

Jet, like amber, is a fossil and has been esteemed for ages; it is a form of coal. The single beads are Iranian, though their source may have been Turkey. The strand is "French jet," really glass most often made in Bohemia.

Keratin

Keratin is a protein in the body of animals which is a constituent of skin and many protective parts. It is soft, yet tough and never stops growing. Our hair and finger and toe nails consist of keratin. So do feathers and bird beaks, porcupine quills, horns and rhino horn (which is really agglutinated hair), claws and hooves and "tortoise shell."

These animal parts have been used for beads for a very long time, and continue to be. Some, such as horn and hooves, are usually cut into beads, while claws and beaks are commonly worn in their natural forms. Rhino horn is not for sale; the rhinoceros is even more endangered than the elephant, but beads had little to do with it, as rhino horn was rarely used for them.

"Tortoise shell" is from yet another endangered species, though old pieces are legal to own. The creature which makes this attractive amber and brown material is not a tortoise, but the hawksbill turtle.

The more expensive keratins, especially "tortoise shell" are widely and easily imitated in plastics. Keratin can be scratched with a knife. In the hot point test it will smell like burning hair, but so will some plastics with certain fillers. Keratin grows in fibers and will chip or flake. If you hold a piece of "tortoise shell" up to the light and look at it with a strong lens the dark area will resolve into many tiny brown dots, something like a half-tone photo in a newspaper.

Lac and Lacquer

These two are easily confused, but are actually quite different. Lac is an Indian product, secreted by small insects to build a nest around the female. Tree branches covered with lac are collected and the lac removed. Traditionally it was colored red from a dye produced from the insect; today aniline dyes are used. Lac has numerous uses; in the purified form it is dissolved in alcohol to make shellac. Lac is a common "paint" in India. Stick lac is used as the base of beads. It chips with a pin and melts with the hot point.

Lacquer is a Chinese and Japanese product made from the sap of a sumac. It is most commonly used to paint or color wood, but can be built up in layers and carved away. Most red "cinnabar" beads on the market are actually lacquer; cinnabar is much heavier. Lac will scratch but not chip with a pin and does not melt with a hot point.

Keratin is an animal protein which makes tough, replaceable body parts. At left are single and double claw pendants from India. Below the double one is a tortoise shell pendant from Veracruz, Mexico. The strand in the middle is made of elephant hair. At top center is a long bead made of water buffalo hoof from Cebu, the Philippines. The two crescent shaped pieces are horn; one is bleached. The strand on the right is made of porcupine quills.

Lac and lacquer are not the same. Lac is an Indian product secreted by an insect used to color wood or serve as the body of an object; shellac is made from it. Lacquer is a Chinese product from a plant sap. The large blue and white beads are lac with decorations stuck in. The large black bead is horn with embedded lac eyes. The round beads at the bottom are Chinese painted with lacquer. The angular ones are Japanese carved from a built-up block of lacquer.

Pearls are the premier bead and have lent their name to the word for bead in many languages. Genuine pearls feel gritty when rubbed gently against the teeth. Artificial ones are big business. The top strand is a good imitation from Japan; the bottom strands are premier imitations from Spain. The white glass bead is the base for better artificial pearls. The large glass half pearl next to it is from Swarovski of Austria. The three to the left are "Roman pearls," made by inflating a glass tube, coating it on the inside with a fish product and filling it with wax. These are no longer made and the specimens here have lost their wax.

The first plastic to be exploited was celluloid, with the disadvantage of being very flammable. It was replaced by a less flammable type in 1926. Turn of the century plastic chains with novelty beads were popular.

Pearls

Pearls are produced by shellfish to coat an irritant in the shell and afford the animal relief. Nearly all shellfish can make pearls, but only a few are of gem quality. They are usually white or slightly gray in color, but natural and cultured pearls of other colors are known; inexpensive ones are often dyed. Pearls are so closely related to beads that the name for beads in several dozen languages is simply the word for pearl.

Pearls have been imitated for a long time in many media. The most successful have been some in glass (see Chapter Seven), but plastics are also widely used. In addition to natural pearls, techniques have been perfected to put a tiny bead into an oyster's shell and let the animal coat the bead for some years, producing a cultured pearl.

Pearls are fragile and should be given special care. They chip easily and should not be stored with other beads. Nor should they be stored in paper, cotton or wood, as they will deteriorate like shell, as discussed in Chapter Two.

The easiest test for pearls is to rub one gently against the underside of your front teeth. Pearls feel gritty, due to the many tiny plates of nacre from which they are formed; imitations do not feel gritty. Perfectly formed pearls that meet this test are virtually all cultured. Perfect, round natural pearls are excessively rare and expensive.

Plastics

Synthetic plastics were first developed in the 1850s and their evolution has brought hundreds of varieties to the present. Plastics are now a global medium for beads. There are over 40 major plastics groups, but the most appealing ones for bead collectors include Celluloid, Casein, Bakelite and Polystyrene.

Celluloid (American trade term; Xylonite in the U.K.) is highly flammable and was replaced by cellulose acetate in 1926. Celluloid has a camphor smell when burned, rubbed against the hand or scratched.

Casein, made from milk (Galalith or "milk stone" is a trade name), was largely a French-German monopoly and is rarely made now. It is hard to mold, so needs to be carved, will slowly absorb a drop of water and often crizzles in humid weather.

Plastic has become a dominant bead material in this century. Many are used for beads, most commonly polystyrene. They can be molded and colored in an endless variety. The large black and white bead is a plastic imitation dZi bead with a metal core to give it heft. The plastic pop bead (orange) is used as money at the vacation resorts of Club Med.

Bakelite is the trade name for phenol formaldehyde, but most "Bakelite" jewelry is actually the pastel shaded urea formaldehyde or the more brightly colored melamine formaldehyde. Bakelite proper is difficult to color except to a black or splotchy amber. This family of plastics was popular in the 1930s for jewelry, often carved. None of them burn.

Polystyrene was invented in 1926 and has become the most common bead plastic. It rings when dropped against a hard surface. When it burns it melts and gives off an orange flame with lots of smoke and soot and a strong acid odor.

In addition to collecting "antique" plastics beads, you might want to look for those made in developing countries. Until World War II, plastic was in the hands of a few industrialized nations. Since then it has become widely used, and many plastic beads are made to suit purely local tastes. Two classes of very collectible beads are made by isolated groups in north and south Philippines. Some Kalinga and T'Boli buy plastic items in the market, melt them and form beads. This is truly a folk art in plastics.

One charm of plastic is that it is fairly simple to make. After World War II the monopoly of industrialized countries was broken and other countries began making plastic for their own markets. The plastic mango leaves can be used in many celebrations in India. The blue beads with red spacers are Turkish for horses and vehicles, replacing glass beads to ward off the Evil Eye. The plastic dZi bead is probably European, but valued in the Himalayas. The other pieces are cut out and glued together in Benaras, India to be worn on the forehead as Tikka.

Thin disc beads can be most attractive when strung together. The black ones at top are Vulcanic beads, made from vulcanized rubber, as is the large red disc. These are popular in some parts of Africa, including among the Mossi of northern Ghana and Burkina Faso. The other beads are later imitations made of plastic. All are probably Czech.

A plastic now sweeping the U.S. is polyform (trade names include Fimo and Sculpey), sometimes called "The New Clay" because it can be worked like clay and hardens readily. The ease of working this material has hundreds of devotees making beads from it (including artists such as Kathleen Duncan, Jamey Allen, and the whimsically named City Zen Cane). The Fimo company in Germany is now turning out premade fancy canes to simplify the making of millefiori and similar beads.

Rose Petals — see Flower Petals

Scented Beads — see Flower Petals

Seeds

Seeds make great beads. A few, like Job's tears and the Chinaberry seed are already perforated or nearly so. Others are easily pierced when fresh or after being soaked in water. The seeds of some palm trees have very white, hard centers and are used for vegetable ivory as an increasingly favored substitute for real ivory.

Hundreds, maybe thousands, of different seeds are being used for beads all around the world, and anyone with an interest in them can build a substantial collection with nothing else. The photographs shown here will help you to identify them.

The story of a couple of bead seeds will illustrate how interesting they are. The most common world-wide bead seed is Job's Tears (*Coix lacryma-jobi*), though technically it is not a seed. Shaped like a tear drop, with a tough, shiny white or gray coating, Job's Tears are nutritious and may have been cultivated before rice in South/Southeast Asia, where they are native. Early farmers may have grown the grain to eat and allowed some to grow wild to furnish beads. It is now found all around the world, and virtually all cultures make beads from it.

The small shiny red seed with a black spot is known by many names, including coral seed (*Abrus precatorius*). It is poisonous, and in India farmers used to make darts from it and shoot it at their neighbor's stray cattle. Coral seed is also consistent enough in size to be used for weighing gold and gems (the English word caret/karat comes from carob seeds, used in this way). Crushed, coral seed produces a glue which jewelers use to temporarily hold small wires or other parts before soldering them. In the last century they were favored in Europe for rosaries. Collect them, but keep them away from children and pets.

Polyform, a type of plastic, often better known by the brand name Fimo, has become a popular medium for professional and amateur beadmakers. The designs which can be worked are unlimited. The spider is by Pat Belcher, the Panda by Gloria Uptain, the star and bead under it by Peter Brisbois and the other four beads by Nan Roche.

By far the most common plant species for beads is the fruit of Job's Tears. Varieties come in different shapes. The natural color is white or gray, such as the loose ones at top from Ghana. Sometime after the 1920s dyeing was perfected, as on the strand imported from Africa with another long seed. The small globular white ones are from the Philippines and the spindle shaped ones (not yet pierced) from northern Thailand.

Many seeds and pods are used for beads around the world. Top left are small brown *Leucaena* seeds. Center left are Chinaberry seeds and to their right a large *Caesalpinia* seed. To its right are some small coral seeds. Bottom left are two water chestnut pods. The strand on the far right is of red *Adenathera* seeds, and to its left a strand with walnut, apricot and peach shells.

Shells

Mollusks are some of the most successful creatures on Earth, being outnumbered only by insects. They inhabit all ecological systems, though none of them fly. Most mollusks protect themselves with a shell, though a few, including the garden slug and the octopus (with the intelligence of a cat) have none.

Young workers piercing shell beads found in the nearby sea at Rameswarem, in southern India.

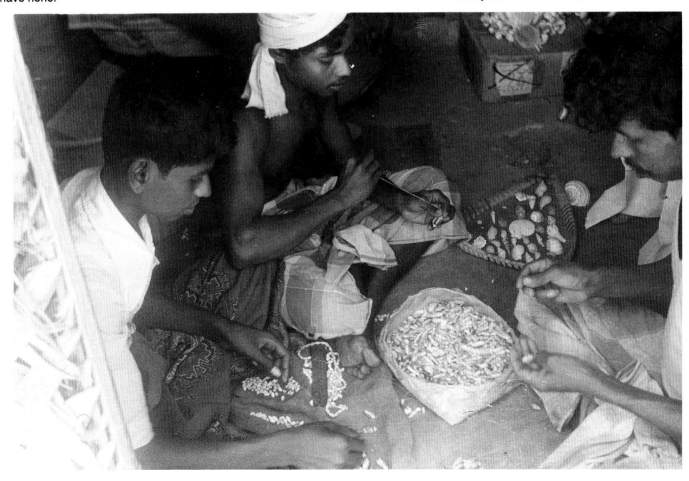

The cowrie shell has been an important bead material since the beginning of time. Center left and right are examples with their backs removed, a typical way to use them. In the center is a large colorful cowrie on a string from Java, Indonesia. On the left are three joined money cowries, and on the right four ring cowries. The strand at the bottom is from the Loimi Akha of northern Thailand with both ring and money cowries interspersed with the seeds of an inedible banana.

The Conus shell, in all its variety, is another important bead shell. Top left and center left are typical Conus top discs from Africa. Top right is a flat species used in New Guinea. Below and to its right is a whole Conus used on a Sioux heirloom necklace. To its right is a cut Conus shell worn in the hair by Mauritanian women, and to its left an imitation in stone. The two shells on the bottom are typical of western Iran around 800 B.C.; one is decorated with a star punched in dots and the other was probably a child's ring.

People have been fascinated by and collectors of sea shells for eons, and they have been making them into beads for nearly as long. Hundreds of shell species are used for beads. Fortunately, there are a number of good books which will help you identify them when they are whole (see the Notes section). To distinguish a bead cut from shell, look closely and turn the bead around until you see three layers, two of which parallel each other and a middle one diagonal to the other two. Shell can be scratched with glass and does not react to the hot point.

One of the most common shell beads is the cowrie. It is often worn by crushing the back of the shell and grinding the rough edge smooth. Cowries remind some people of women and others of eyes. They once reminded some Italians of little pigs, and their Italian name *porcellana* came to be attached to the similarly shiny white ceramic exported from China. Cowries have functioned as small change in many places, especially the money cowrie, which has a limited natural range.

The tops of Conus shells are another very popular bead. The carnivorous Conus snail reabsorbs the central supporting column most snails have and the shell is thus hollow. Break off the base of the shell, grind the edge smooth and grind the apex until a hole is made to form a disc that can be used in many styles of jewelry. Conus shells, too, have an ancient pedigree and are still widely used; there are even imitations in glass.

Tortoise Shell — see Keratin

Wood

Woods of all sorts are made into beads all around the world. Many such beads are painted, dyed or covered with lac, shellac or varnish, and the original surface is hidden.

One wood favored for beads is quite expensive: the sweet smelling heart of the sandalwood tree. Essence can be soaked in other sorts of wood, but true sandalwood has a yellow color which is not common in other woods.

In addition to wood proper, some woody products, such as seed capsules, bamboo sections (bamboo is actually a grass) and cork (the bark of a tree) are used for beads. Most of these can be recognized, though someone may have to help you make the initial identification.

A hot point test on the wood will smell like burning wood. Wood also has characteristic grains. Some woods, such as palm with its thick vascular bundles, making a dotted pattern on the end, are fairly easy to recognize, while many others require an expert's help.

A woman making wooden beads in a suburb of Channapatna, India. She has drilled a wooden dowel, held by her feet, which she is now segmenting into beads. Later they will be colored with lac.

Wood and wood products have been used for beads from the beginning. The single center bead is cork, a tree bark. The thin beads under it are bamboo, made by young men in Ghana to give to their girlfriends. The larger round beads colored with lac are made by women in a suburb of Channapatna, India.

The Eucalyptus tree provides several beads around the world, even though native to Australia. The woody seed pods at left were perforated in West Africa. Caps are formed by the petals before the tree flowers; the small conical ones in the center are strung by girls in central Mexico, the large rough ones, some of which are dyed, are from Australia.

CHAPTER FIVE
STONE BEADS

Stones, or more properly rocks and minerals, make some of the most attractive and enchanting beads. Their durability and beauty have placed them in the forefront of desired and valuable beads through the ages. In fact, the most expensive single bead is of stone: an antique jade pendant sold at auction in Hong Kong for nearly a million dollars.

Before the introduction of techniques to facet gemstones, nearly all precious stones were made into beads. The Romans thought nothing of wearing drilled emeralds, and ancient Indians and Chinese made neck-laces of drilled rubies. Diamond, the hardest natural substance, was not made into beads quite as early; its primary use for a long time was as a tool, as a drill bit for boring beads. The majority of stone beads we encounter, however, are made from semiprecious or even more prosaic stones.

The word "stone" is a general and non-scientific term. Stones are either minerals, with distinct chemical combinations, or rocks, which are a mixture of minerals. Most popular stone beads are minerals, but some, such as lapis lazuli, are rocks.

Collecting stone beads has a double advantage. Not only are there bead collectors who specialize in stones, but there is also a large group of people who collect stones. Many of them concentrate on mineral crystals or other exotica not immediately related to beads, but the material is all the same. As a result, there is a large body of literature to help you identify troublesome stone beads and many local "rockhound" groups which can serve as resources.

IDENTIFYING BEAD STONES

Virtually every mineral and rock has been made into a bead at some time, from diamonds to salt cubes. To identify stones, get a good mineral book, study it and learn how to perform the diagnostic tests. The initial task is to look at the bead and note its color and luster.

The first test you will learn is for hardness (H) or the relative ability of a mineral to scratch another one. All minerals are assigned a number from one (talc, the softest) to ten (diamond, the hardest). A sample set of minerals with constant hardness can be used to test an unknown mineral. Some everyday objects are also useful to remember: fingernails are H 2.5, a copper penny H 3, a pen knife blade H 5, ordinary glass H 5.5, and a steel file H 6.5. So, for example, a bead that scratches a penny but is scratched by a knife blade is about H 4.

Rocks and minerals from all over the world lend their colors to popular beads. At left is a pendant of black opal from Australia. The strands are: zoisite from Tanzania; lapis lazuli chips from Afghanistan; yellow jasper cornerless cubes from India; and amethyst chips from India. The heart is malachite.

In ancient times, the best way to hold onto wealth was to wear it. Precious materials of all sorts were made into beads. The brownish stones are zircon and the reddish ones garnet. In the center is a beryl. The small pearls are natural; notice their uneven shapes.

A useful test that requires a piece of equipment is for specific gravity or the denseness of the bead. For this you need an accurate scale; almost any type will work. You weigh the bead, then weigh it again while it is suspended in water (put the bead on a string, first dipping it into water and blowing through the hole to prevent air being trapped). Subtract the wet weight from the dry weight and divide the difference into the dry weight to arrive at the specific gravity.

If you get more involved, you might want to add ultraviolet lights to test for fluorescence, a refractometer and a polariscope. Some of these tests are also useful for certain types of glasses. But, you need not spend much money on the more simple tests, and depending upon your interests, many collectors will get along with a minimum of equipment.

Some Important Bead Stones

By far the most used minerals for beads are members of the quartz family. They come in a wide variety of colors and patterns and are made into beads because of their availability, beauty and durability. The quartz family consists of four groups: crystalline quartz, chalcedony, jasper, and opal. All chemically similar, they differ in the arrangements of their crystals. Each group has a variety of species within it, mostly defined by color.

Crystalline quartz forms large, visible six-sided crystals. Most species are transparent and glassy in luster; rock crystal (clear), amethyst (purple), citrine (golden), smoky quartz (gray to brown) and rose quartz (pink) are the best known members. Inclusions make other varieties: Venus hair (with rutile crystals), aventurine (with various glittering specks) and tiger eye (with asbestos). Quartz is the standard for Hardness 7; it will scratch most anything except the more precious gems (garnet, topaz, ruby, diamond).

Chalcedony (the agate group). These are formed of tiny microcrystals, arranged in a fibrous manner. The members are translucent, arranged in bands (look closely), have a greasy luster and a hardness of 6.5 (can be scratched with difficulty by a quartz crystal). When this material is white to blue-gray it is called chalcedony. Carnelian is the red variety; sard the brown. When there are more than one color it is usually called agate: banded, moss (with mineral inclusions) and several hundred other named types.

The crystalline quartz group consists of minerals which form large crystals. These include purple amethyst (strand from India), rose quartz (cube from Mexico), and rock crystal (center one is modern Indian; others are older).

Chalcedony is a common form of microcrystalline quartz. It is virtually homogeneous, unlike banded forms classified as agates. Most are referred to by their color, except the red, which is called carnelian. The blue is rare. The heart is modern Indian, the others, older Indian from Iran.

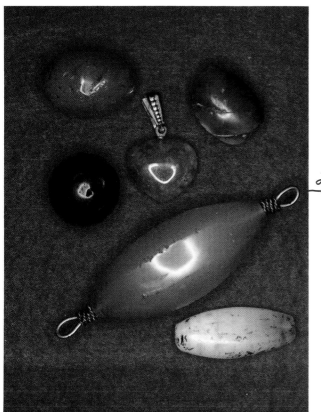

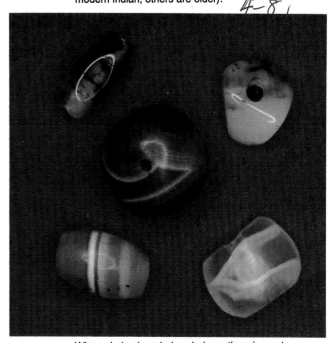

When chalcedony is banded or otherwise patterned it is called agate. The moss agate bead at upper left and the white agate beads at upper right are modern Indian. The other beads were collected in Iran.

The other major microcrystalline quartz family is jasper, distinguished by being opaque. It is usually referred to by color: red, green, yellow, etc. White or gray jasper is called flint or chert. The cube with the corners ground off is used against the Evil Eye. All beads collected in Iran except the long faceted red jasper one, from Egypt.

As the most common mineral, the varieties of quartz are almost endless. The strand is a rock with a quartz base cementing pieces of pyrite. The round bead is bloodstone, green jasper with flecks of red. The odd shaped bead is tiger-eye, which shimmers because of included asbestos.

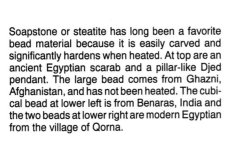

Jasper also forms as microcrystals, but they are granular rather than fibrous. Jasper is opaque except on the thinnest edges, has a waxy luster and a hardness of 6.5. Instead of the Babel of names agate has, jaspers are usually just called red, green, brown or yellow. White or black jasper is called flint or chert.

Opal has even smaller crystals in an unusual spherical form. Common opal is milky white; precious opal displays flashes of color due to entrapped water. Opal is expensive, and buying it requires a trusted dealer. It is not widely used for beads because it beaks rather easily. Its hardness is about 5.5.

Another very important mineral is steatite, also called soapstone. This strange material is an impure form of talc, easily scratched with your fingernail, and commonly carved into fancy shapes. When heated, it hardens, often considerably, up to H 5.5 or even 6.5. Opaque and otherwise dull black, white, sometimes green or red beads which have been elaborately and effortlessly carved are most commonly made of steatite.

Soapstone or steatite has long been a favorite bead material because it is easily carved and significantly hardens when heated. At top are an ancient Egyptian scarab and a pillar-like Djed pendant. The large bead comes from Ghazni, Afghanistan, and has not been heated. The cubical bead at lower left is from Benaras, India and the two beads at lower right are modern Egyptian from the village of Qorna.

Soapstone comes in a variety of natural colors and will take a dye, though not too successfully. The large oval piece is a greenish scarab blank from Egypt. The other beads are from Mexico, the white one natural and the others dyed purple and blue.

Jade is an expensive but very important bead material. Two different minerals with similar properties are called jade: jadeite and nephrite. Nephrite is the traditional jade of China, while jadeite from Burma was introduced later. In the New World, jadeite was the stone of choice; it was so highly valued that Montezuma told Cortez that a single jadite bead he gave him was worth 100 pounds of gold.

Jadeite is tough to carve, has a hardness of about 6.5 and a greasy luster that polishes glassy. The most celebrated color is spinach green. Nephrite is slightly softer but also quite tough. It comes in a variety of colors, but white is common; the most valuable was yellow, reserved for the Chinese emperor. Both have tiny pits visible on the surface, and unpolished jadeite looks quite rough. Imitations in other stones and glass abound. As with all precious stones, buy only when you are sure.

Jade may be either of two minerals and comes in many colors. The square pieces to be sewn onto clothing are jadeite; notice the very rough surface on the unpolished side. The small round beads are nephrite. The ring shaped pendant is glass, and the large sew-on flower at bottom is serpentine. All are Chinese.

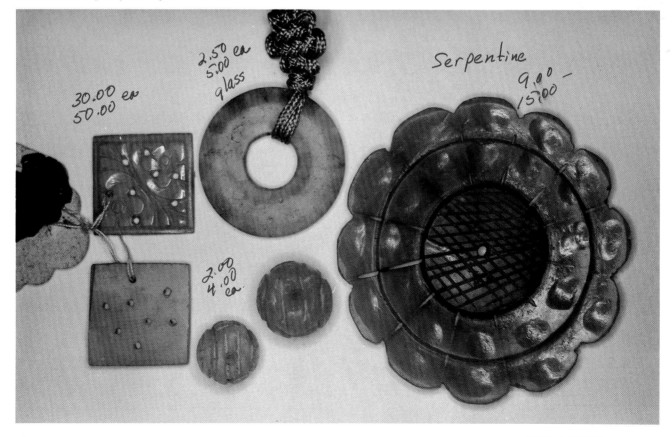

Lapis lazuli is a rock rather than a mineral. The blue lazurite has long been highly prized. It is typically mixed with calcite (white) and flecks of pyrite (fools' gold). The ancient pieces here are of varying qualities; the modern bead at bottom center is of good quality.

Although the list of stone beads is endless, the last one we shall mention is a rock: lapis lazuli. Prized for thousands of years, the only known ancient source is in northern Afghanistan. Its blue color inspired many ancient imitations in faience and glass; in the Middle Ages it was the source for ultramarine blue for painters. Lapis lazuli consists of lazurite, the blue mineral, pyrite (fool's gold), which give it distinctive golden specks, and calcite, the white "matrix." The deeper the blue, the better the stone. Dying is a common practice.

MAKING STONE BEADS

To make beads from stones a certain amount of technical knowledge is necessary, which is why there were few stone beads in the Old Stone Age. Stone beadmaking technology can be traced step by step throughout time, though there have been many variations. The traditional techniques outlined here are those used by the stone beadmakers of Cambay, India. Observations are also made about the large industry in Idar-Oberstein, Germany. Other differences are noted among other industries I have observed.

One must begin with raw material. This can be found locally or imported from some distance. The value of the material will depend upon its purity and the scarcity of the particular stone. It may come in the form of large chunks cut from a mountain side, boulders gathered in a river bed, or smaller pieces dug from old deposits or dredged from a river.

The first step is to cut away the unwanted parts of the stone and get down to fine, smaller pieces that can be worked into beads. This is usually done by chipping the stone. In Cambay a worker braces the stone against the tip of an iron stake and hits it with a hammer of water buffalo horn mounted on a bamboo. Other methods, such as a hammer and chisel are possible, and one can chip stones with other stones. The crude protobead is called a roughout.

Large pieces of raw material can also be cut into slabs with a saw. This has been done for centuries in China, where the treadle was invented to provide power from the feet. Most Mexican stone beadmakers use small diamond saws to cut smaller and smaller pieces. Some mechanized Asian beadmakers use a series of saws to cut the material into slabs, then pencils and then cubes.

Roughouts are next ground into a final shape. This can be done any number of ways. Emery secured on wooden plates with lac are used in Cambay. Commercial lapidary wheels are used by other stone beadmakers. In the last century, huge sandstone wheels driven by water power were used at Idar-Oberstein and men had to lie on their stomachs to reach them to grind the stones in their hands. A finished ground stone is called a blank.

The sources for ornamental stones are varied. This man is at the entrance to a shaft dug into the ground to extract agates and carnelians near Ratanpur, India.

Steps in making a carnelian stone bead. A raw pebble from the mines in Ratanpur, India, is brown or dark in color. It is chipped into a roughout and then ground into a blank. Perforating, polishing and heating to bring out the red color follow.

Stones are chipped into roughouts in Cambay, India. The stone is braced against an iron stake and hit with a hammer made of water buffalo horn and bamboo.

The blank is then drilled. Drilling is usually done from both sides; if not, the far end will chip out before the hole is complete. In Cambay they still use bow drills and drill one end, then turn the bead around and drill the other. This often results in holes not well aligned (you can straighten them with a thin file or small drill). In Idar-Oberstein a drill press is used, which results in straighter holes. Many beadmakers now have electric drills; ultrasound is increasingly being used.

Double tipped diamond drills, which leave thin, straight holes, have been used in the Indian industry for well over 2000 years. Before that, beads had to be drilled with stone drills or copper or wooden drills with abrasives. Those older holes are larger and also hourglass-shaped in profile.

The last step is polishing, traditionally done in one of two ways. Round beads were tumbled by being put into a bag with some water and agate dust and rolled along the floor between two men for two weeks. Faceted beads were polished by hand against a hard wood or bamboo or a metal plate. Today the tumbling is mechanized, and nearly all Indian faceted beads are also being tumbled.

Understanding these techniques can provide hints to the age of stone beads in your collection. Boring with double tipped diamond drills does not go back much more than 2300 years or so. Most faceted beads which have been polished by hand rather than being tumbled are probably 1000 or more years old, except for complex multifaceted ones, which lose their character if they are tumbled, and are hand faceted even to this day.

The drilling of ground stone blanks is still done with a bow drill in and around Cambay, India. The pot with the thin tube drips water onto the bead and drill to keep them cool.

Coloring Stones

Most people are surprised to learn that it is possible to color stones. In fact, the coloring of stones goes back a very long time and in many cases is so well established that it is no longer considered necessary to inform a buyer that some alteration has taken place.

The most common bead stone which is usually artificially colored is the great favorite, *carnelian*. Carnelian is a form of chalcedony, the same family to which agate belongs. When raw stones are dug up in Ratanpur ("the Village of Gems"), India, for sale to Cambay, the preferred stones are dark brown or olive in color. How do they become red? Due to the nature of the deposits around this village, the stones have been sitting in a layer of silt heavy in iron. The stone slowly absorbed this iron, and when the beadmaker has finished a bead he heats it in a muffled (oxygen starved) furnace. The dark iron turns red.

Idar-Oberstein, Germany, developed into a major beadmaking center beginning around 1820. The raw materials come from all over the world, but the quartz group of beads are mostly from Minas Gerais, Brazil, whose uncolored chalcedony is especially porous and dyes easily. The large carnelian seen here on the left is typical of older work, with a dusky hue and finely ground surfaces. The onyx beads are newer and have been tumbled rather than hand polished.

Onyxes of various types and dates. All were collected in Iran, though probably made in India. Notice how skillfully they were cut to reveal natural patterns in the stone. The one on bottom right is a sardonyx, heated to bring out the red color, but not subjected to further treatment to turn some bands brown or black.

Carnelians from Idar-Oberstein undergo a different process. The Germans get their raw material from Brazil, where a particularly porous chalcedony is available in Minas Gerais state. To make carnelian, this stone is soaked in an acid bath into which iron has been dissolved. After a few weeks the stone will contain enough iron to turn red upon heating.

Also common in collections are *onyx* beads. Onyx is Greek for fingernail, giving its name to the stone because of its bands of color. There is no real difference between onyx and banded agate, except that the onyx has been treated. In one method, the agate has been soaked in a sugar solution for a few weeks, and the more porous gray or brown bands absorb the sugar. When the stone is later heated, the sugar is caramelized and a brown and white onyx results. In the other method, the stone has been put in sulfuric acid and the sugar carbonized, making a black and white onyx.

There are many other ways of coloring stones, and some of them are quite old. *Citrine* (golden quartz) is nearly always made by heating poor quality amethyst, a system invented some 2000 years ago. But most of these techniques are newer. Idar-Oberstein has become famous for giving every conceivable shade to the porous Brazilian chalcedony. Within the field of precious stones, the practice has become a scandal, as rubies and sapphires are treated to improve their color, emeralds bathed in green oil to conceal their faults, and totally unnatural stones, such as the blue topaz, are created.

What is a poor bead collector to do? Fortunately, since most stone beads are semiprecious, you will not lose a lot of money buying something that is not what you think (hope). Since carnelian and onyx hardly exist in the natural state, and their treatments are so ancient, no one is concerned about them. Stones which are simply dyed on the surface — howalite posing for turquoise — can be checked with acetone (see Chapter Four). Stones which are given double names — new Jade, Korea jade, Suzhou jade, Swiss lapis, smoky topaz — are nearly always something else. This even applies to "Brazil topaz," which is the much cheaper citrine, even though Brazil is the world's major supplier of true topaz. The only real protection is to study your stones and buy from someone who is honest and will be open with you.

Patterning Stones

People are never quite satisfied with what they have, no matter how attractive. Thus it was from an early date some were decorating stones in different ways to produce various patterns. Many of these techniques are quite old and some of their products are among the most interesting of beads.

The first decorating to be used was the glazing of stone, done in Egypt and Sudan 5500 or so years ago. Steatite and quartz (including amethyst) were most widely used. By adding an alkali to the surface and heating the bead, the alkali and the silica of the stone would react to form a thin layer of glass or glaze. Copper was commonly included to impart the desired blue color to the stone to imitate lapis lazuli and/or turquoise. Some authorities believe there is a historical connection between glazing stones and glassmaking.

Also very early was the adding of patterns in white onto dark stones, usually carnelians. Although this is commonly referred to as "etching," no acid is involved. Rather an alkali, soda or potash, was painted onto the bead and the bead was heated for a short time. The alkali penetrated the surface of the bead and spread out under the surface, leaving an indelible white line. Sometimes the whole bead was covered with alkali to make it white and black lines drawn on the white with manganese, or more rarely, directly on the red.

The history of "etched carnelians" is complex. They are first recorded in the Harappan or Indus Valley Civilization of India and Pakistan about 2400 B.C. This is not surprising, as this society had mastered the patterning and altering of many stones. Patterns rarely found in India were much more common in Sameria (modern Iraq) at the same time, and it seems they made these beads, too. Around 2000 years ago Persians (in modern Iran) also learned how to make patterned beads. Unusual patterns in Thailand at about this time suggest the transfer of technology there as well, whereas different patterns in northern and southern India indicate more than one center of production.

Interestingly, both the glazing of quartz and the "etching" of carnelian were continued in Iran for a long time. Even after the coming of Islam to the country, the beads were still made, many of the "etched" carnelians being traded to the Viking world along with silver in exchange for dried fish, furs, honey and wax and amber. In time, beads were no longer produced, but carnelian plaques were decorated with passages from the Qoran or other pious sayings. Only in this century has etching ceased in Iran; acid is now employed to make these ornamental plaques. The making of "etched" carnelians also continued in Pakistan until the beginning of this century.

When the technology of darkening chalcedony or agates was wedded to that of "etching" the result was a bead usually black all over with white patterned lines. These are commonly known as *dZi* beads (variously spelled) and are quite popular, scarce and expensive. Before the bead was blackened, the areas to be later "etched" were left blank by adding a resist (such as grease) to the surface to prevent those areas from turning black. No one yet knows where and when dZi beads were made. The techniques for making them date back in India about 3500 years, but the earliest beads treated this way (though without the usual dZi bead patterns) are only about 2000 years old.

The patterning of stones, so common within the Indianized world, was also done in ancient Burma by the Pyu, who were heavily influenced by Indian culture. They used fossilized wood onto which they put patterns. These beads became heirlooms and are now called Pumtek. In this century they have been imitated. Their story is told more fully in Chapter Ten.

Carnelians which have been given designs by means of adding an alkali are usually called "etched," though no acid is involved. The smooth lines are indelible. The center bead was bought in Egypt and may be the oldest of the group. The others are from India or Iran, some 1500 to 2000 years old.

CHAPTER SIX
GLASS BEADS

Glass is the premier bead material. It can be worked into many shapes, colors and sizes. These are small drawn "seed beads" on a necklace. The colors of the light green and white are in the glass; the dark green beads have been lined with paint.

Glass has been the most important bead material for thousands of years. It is fairly inexpensive to make, can be formed into almost any shape in an extremely wide pallet of colors and is reasonably durable and hard. Glass is a most peculiar substance however, a fact we rarely consider.

Glass is not really a solid but a supercooled liquid, which some would classify as a state of matter all its own. Glass is made by melting crystalline substances and cooling them below the point where they would crystallize, but not letting this happen. It can be made from almost any metal or metalloid, but by far the most common one is silica, the basis of quartz, usually in the form of sand.

Glass was first invented in the Middle East about 2500 B.C. For a long time, it was a wonder and the secrets of its production were not easily revealed. It was first used for beads, and they were widely traded. Eventually the craft came to be at home in many different places. China and India invented glass independently of each other and the Middle East around 1100 B.C.

Ancient furnaces were not hot enough to melt silica, and so an ingredient to help it melt (called a flux) was added. This was usually soda or another alkali, derived from plant ashes or deposits such as at the Dead Sea or Lake Natron in Egypt. Silica and alkali alone make glass, but it is unstable and will dissolve in water. A stabilizer is needed, most commonly lime. It seems that early glassmakers did not know this, but lime was always introduced accidentally along with the sand. The sand and alkali are fired for a couple of weeks and the result is an unpromising hard gray material called frit. This is broken up, pieces of older glass added to it, and the whole fired again before molten glass flows in the furnace.

Glassmaking is not the same as glassworking. Once glass is made, it is relatively easy to melt down and form into anything one wants. By no means are all beadmakers glassmakers. Many rely upon glass made by someone else, either in the form of scrap glass, such as broken bottles, or products especially made for them, including ingots called cakes and rods called canes. In Medieval Europe, for example, some beadmakers simply used glass mosaic tiles originally designed to decorate floors and walls.

The way in which glass beads were made is an important clue to identifying their origin. While some methods are widely used, others are employed only by certain beadmakers. In the chapters that follow, most glass beads will be described by the method used to make them, so the material in this chapter is important in identifying the origins of beads.

MAKING BEADS

Winding

The oldest and most universal way to make a glass bead is to work with hot glass and wrap it around a shaft of some sort to build up the bead. This circular motion should be kept in mind, because the finished bead will nearly always reveal this twisting action. Any imperfections in the glass, streaks in color or air bubbles, will be oriented so they encircle the perforation. We call these *wound beads*. There are several ways to wind beads, but there are some techniques common to each.

A bead being wound can be shaped or decorated as long as it remains hot. Simply keeping it in the heat and twirling the rod it is on will round it off through centrifugal force. Beadmakers use a flat paddle to shape the bead, making it more round, cubical, flat or whatever. The edge of this tool can

Winding glass beads directly from the furnace. This boy in Purdalpur, India has wound the beads on his iron mandrel and is now giving them a rounded shape with a small tool.

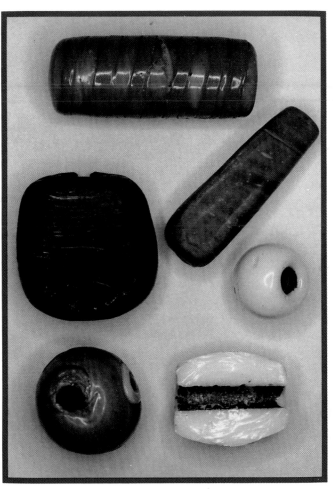

Furnace-wound glass beads. The beads are made by twirling hot glass in a crucible in a furnace around an iron rod. Still on the rod the bead can be shaped with a paddle or glass can be added to decorate it. After the bead is heated the last time, it is knocked off the iron rod, which contracts a little faster than the glass upon cooling. A thin coating of black iron oxide is left in the perforation.

make incisions or other motifs. A second color of glass can be added (both glasses must be kept hot), or several colors put next to each other or on top of each other. The paddle can work the design around by dragging through it. This is called "combing," and will form waves or feather decorations from lines or floral motifs from dots. Wound beads need to be cooled slowly or annealed to prevent the beads from cracking.

Furnace-winding is done by poking an iron rod into the hot glass in a crucible in the furnace. The bead is wound up in the furnace, then removed and any modifications to it are made. When the bead is done, a final heating makes it red hot and then it can be knocked off the iron rod because the iron contracts slightly faster than the glass as they cool. The bead is usually knocked into a small chamber attached to the furnace for annealing, staying in and cooling off for several hours. Furnace-wound beads typically have fairly wide perforations and a thin layer of black iron oxide inside from the iron rod.

Lamp-winding begins with semi-finished glass products called canes, which are rods of glass furnished by the glassmaker. The worker sits at a table with a jet of fire (the lamp) in front, the cane in one hand and a wire in another. The glass cane is gently heated until it begins to slump and is then wound around the wire. The bead is shaped with a paddle or other glass rods or elements are added to decorate it. The bead may be spun in an open half-mold or a trough to give it a more perfectly rounded shape. When it is finished it is often flame-annealed, put in the slightly cooler end of the flame until it is sooty, then set aside. To remove the bead from the wire it is usual to coat the wire with a separator. Many different compounds can be used for this; kaolin clay is a common example. Lamp-wound beads are often more decoratively complex than furnace-wound ones, will have smaller holes and often some powdery separator, at least when the bead is new.

Lamp-winding in the 1600s. The women are using an oil lamp and tools (pictured below them) to make beads. Note the large vent. From Antonio Neri's *L'arte Vetraria*, plate IX.

Lamp-wound beads are made by heating preformed rods of glass, called canes, at a table and winding the hot glass around a wire. Shaping may be done with a paddle. Round beads can be shaped by spinning them in a small half-mold while still on the wire, as is done in several places (the two right beads from India were finished this way). Venetians rounded their beads with a tong mold or rolled them down a small trough, which leaves some of the wound structure at the ends, as on the two beads second from right. A coating is usually put on the wire to allow the bead to slip off, leaving a perforation deposit as seen in the broken black bead.

There are a couple of minor winding techniques. *Scoop-winding* takes glass from the furnace on a scoop and trails it over a rod, which is then put back in the furnace to rework the bead. This method is used by a few small Middle Eastern beadmakers. *Drip-winding* is the heating of canes or glass scrap, dripping the glass over a wire or rod which has to be turned to wind the bead. Often the glass is not very hot and small peaks are left on the ends of the beads; this is a common Far Eastern technique.

Drawing

Drawing is the other major beadmaking technique. The beadmaker begins with a fairly large gather of glass which is made hollow by any one of several means (blowing is one). Then the hollow glass is stretched out (drawn) into a long tube, which often does not need to be annealed. The drawing can be done by one man alone or the tube can be pulled out between two workers. Since 1917 the machine invented by Edward Danner of the Libby Glass Company has made tube drawing automatic, and these machines or variations of them have been placed in use around the world.

The glass can be decorated before it is drawn out. Rods of glass along the side will make lines on the final bead. Two or more layers of glass may make up the original gather, resulting in beads with a core. The most complex of these beads have several different layers, each cog-shaped, which is done by successive molding before the tube is drawn out. The end result is the famous chevron bead, which is then ground on the ends or heated and pinched to show the cog design as a row of chevron zig-zags.

A master in the village of Purdalpur, India, prepares a glass gather which he will later inflate through the blowpipe and draw alone into a long tube.

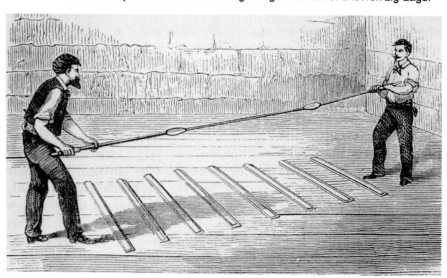

The drawing of a (rather short) tube by two men as depicted in *Harper's* in 1871 (Abbott 1871:353).

DRAWING OUT A GLASS TUBE.

The drawn tube becomes the basis for the beads. After it has been cut into yard (meter) long lengths, it is further chopped up into smaller pieces. These can be left as is, though they will be sharp at the ends. They are more commonly packed in some powder that will not melt or react with the glass and stirred or rotated over heat for a short time. This action softens the beads and they melt at the ends, rounding them off. Beads made this way are called *drawn beads*. They are distinguished by being relatively uniform and having the glass, air bubbles, and usually the decoration running parallel to the perforation. Small glass "seed" beads for beadwork are made this way. So are many other well-known beads.

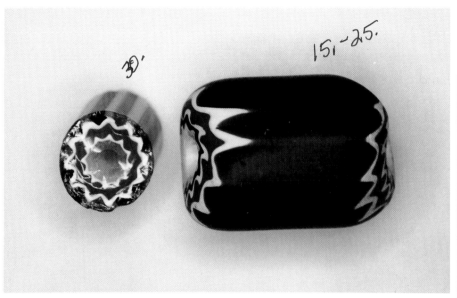

Chevron beads are great favorites with most collectors. They are drawn beads made from tubes with multiple layers, at least some of which are molded into cogwheel patterns before being drawn out.

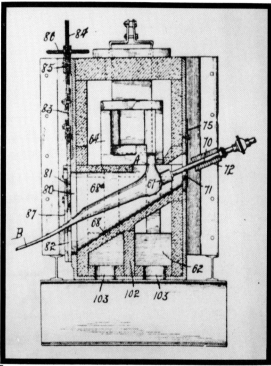

Sketch of a patent of 1917 taken out by Edward Danner for a machine to automatically draw glass tubes, which revolutionized beadmaking. The glass at A comes out of a heating chamber onto a hollow mandrel, which continually blows air, producing a tube at B as the glass slips off the mandrel.

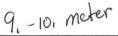

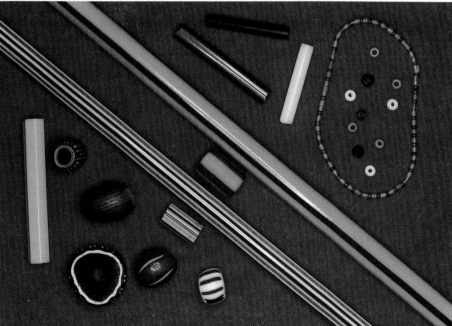

Drawn glass beads are made from plain or multilayered tubes pulled or drawn out, then cut apart. The finished beads may be left as tubes, rounded off by tumbling, heated and pinched off the tube, cut into discs or treated other ways. Small beads used for beadwork are drawn. All beads are probably Venetian.

Molding

There are many ways of shaping glass in simple molds, and this is sometimes done to wound beads. However, true molding is a method which has become increasingly important only in the last two centuries. A bit of hot glass, usually a cane heated in a lamp, is put into a mold which closes on it and forms a bead. Some provision must be made for a short rod to pierce the bead for the perforation. When the mold is opened the bead is taken out. Some of the hot glass seeps between the halves of the mold, leaving flash or a seam line, which is usually removed later. On more expensive beads the flash may be ground off manually; on more common ones it is tumbled off. Molded beads often have complex designs and small holes, though some of the earlier ones may differ. They always have a seam, visible as a dark line, a ridge, an interruption of a pattern or a ground girdle.

A special type of molding is known as Prosser, after the brothers Richard and Thomas Prosser who invented the machine to accomplish this molding by 1840. The machine subjects a pellet of clay mixed with other ingredients to great pressure in a die. The pressure vitrifies (makes into glass) the clay, and the finished bead is quite exact in form. Prosser beads will have seams, but they are hard to spot. On round Prosser beads the seams are hidden at one edge of an equatorial zone (sometimes they have been tumbled away). On cylindrical beads (tile beads) and interlocking beads the seams are along one edge. Prosser beads are also recognized by having one shiny and smooth end and the opposite end pitted like an orange peel.

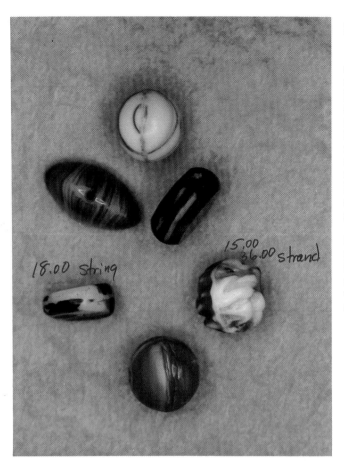

Molded glass beads will show a seam somewhere on the bead. It may be more or less obvious, will sometimes interrupt a design or can be removed by grinding (as the dark blue bead) or tumbling. All beads are Czech.

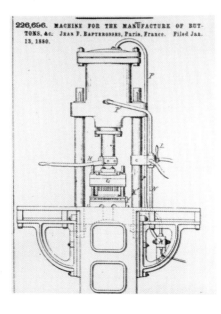

Sketch from a 1880 patent by Jean Felix Bapterosses for improvements in the Prosser machine. Clay pellets were subjected to great pressure to make beads and buttons.

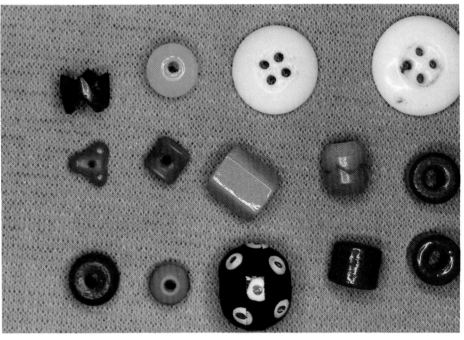

The Prosser brothers invented a button making machine in the 1830s. It subjected a clay mixture to great pressure to turn it into glass. The buttons are commonly called "china buttons." By the 1860s improvements, mostly from France, expanded the products to include beads. Prosser beads always have a thin seam hidden on an edge, are uniform in shape and size, of opaque or cloudy glass and have one shiny and one pitted end (compare the two brown beads at right). Many beads were made by this process, especially in Bohemia and France. Round ones usually have a thick equatorial band (note the black eye bead). Short cylinders (brown beads) are called "tile beads." Most interlocking beads are made this way.

Blowing

Beads can also be made by inflating a thin tube into a bead shape. The tube must first be drawn, then the bead can be made. Some beads are made free-hand, while others are blown into a mold designed to make many beads at one time. These thin beads may be cut apart or left attached to each other. Beads decorating Christmas trees are made this way. Often they are further decorated by being coated inside with silver or other colors. Certain imitation "Roman" pearls were made like this (see Chapter Seven, France). These beads are fragile, but easily identified by their hollow centers.

Blowing glass beads makes a fragile, light product. The three beads in the center are probably all Czech and have been ground to reveal interior layers. The two leaf shaped beads to the left were free-blown. The small beads on the right were blown in molds.

After tubes are molded into a series of bulges to be cut apart into beads, workers in Firozbad, India suck silver ammonia nitrate into the tubes to give them a silver lining. The practice is not recommended.

DECORATING GLASS BEADS

A number of bead decorating techniques have already been mentioned when discussing various ways of making beads. The important thing to remember is that glass beads are almost never painted, as some are apt to say, but are decorated with other colors of glass. Lines added to a bead are usually referred to as *trailed* lines. Colors atop colors, such as for eye beads, are known as *stratified* decorations. Decorations caused by dragging the edge of a tool through lines or dots is known as *combing*.

One of the more complex and interesting decorations is done by adding prepared fancy elements to the surface of a bead. When the whole bead is covered with these elements we call it a *millefiori* (Italian for "a thousand flowers") or a *mosaic* bead. These elements are made by the drawing technique; they are canes without holes in the center, made of several colors of glass arranged in some pattern. After they are drawn out into long canes they are cut up into short pieces, which are placed individually onto the body of a (usually wound) bead. The fancy patterns can be made in several ways: unicolored rods may be bunched together; hot strips of glass can be laid atop one another; the glass can be coated with different colors of glass to make a bullseye effect; the layers can be molded like chevrons; or a combination can be used.

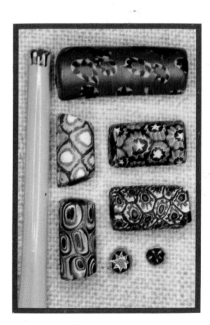

Mosaic or millefiori beads are wound bead decorated with thin slices of multilayered or patterned drawn canes. There are several ways to make such patterns. The large orange bead, the blue cane slice and the yellow cane are Indian; the patterns have been built up one color at a time while the glass is kept hot. Star arms and flower petals are independent of one another. The bead with the white stars and the orange cane slice have had their patterns molded; they are Venetian from 1920 on. The lower right bead and the top bullseye bead have had their patterns produced by bundling individual canes, Venetian pre-1920s. The bullseye pattern at bottom has been built with colored layers, Venetian.

10.00-25.00

Satin glass is made by purposely introducing bubbles into the glass. When the tube is drawn out the bubbles elongate and produce a satiny effect. The pits on the end of the large blue bead are air holes, most of which go through the length of the bead. Mostly Czech, where they are called "Atlas" glass.

Beads may be given coatings for a surface finish. The six smaller beads were coated with an organic lacquer mixed with metal. The lacquer is burned off leaving an effect often called "iris." The two larger beads have relatively thick coatings for a pearly look.

One way to finish glass beads is to give them a matte or frosted surface. This can be done by careful tumbling, but is more often done with a bath in hydrofluoric acid.

The glass from which a bead is made can be special in several ways: the bead may be made of two or more layers of glass; one color of glass layered over another is called "casing." Thin rods of glass may be placed in a dominant transparent glass to give the finished bead a filigree or other effect. Satin glass is made by having numerous tiny air bubbles stretched out through the glass. Other special glasses are known as opal glass, with tiny crystals which give it an opalescent effect, and goldstone or aventurine, as discussed below.

After beads are made they can be given a further finish. Some are simply heated, which smooths out the surface and gives a shiny "fire polish." Other beads are dipped in hydrofluoric acid or tumbled with an abrasive, which gives them a matte or frosted finish. Beads can be coated with materials that make them shimmer like pearls. They can be also covered with a lacquer of organic and metal compounds. When heated, the organic material burns away, leaving a thick metallic coating. In a more sophisticated manner, metal ions are vaporized to coat the bead with a surface thin enough to interfere with a wave of light. This breaks up the light and imparts a rainbow effect. The most famous of these is known as *Aurora Borealis*, and its cousin with a thinner coat, the colder and more dramatic *Glacier Blue*.

Glass beads can also be coated or lined on the inside. This is done on transparent beads so the coating shows out through the glass. Blown beads are often silvered inside the perforation. Even many simple small drawn "seed beads" are lined with paint. Lining gives the beads special visual effects, but will fade or wear out over time.

Another way to decorate glass beads is to facet them after they have been made. These are often called "cut beads," but not all so-called cut beads are the same. The term applies to faceted beads, but some are only faceted by being drawn into tubes with six or so sides. Others are wound beads with facets applied by the beadmaker's paddle. Still others have facets because the bead was molded that way.

True hand faceting is usually applied only to better beads. Many beads are first formed in molds and then faceted by hand against a wheel. Better beads cut this way are sometimes called "tin cut," from the material of the wheel. Some beads have both molded and ground facets on them, which is usually the case with "Vaseline" beads. A very popular bead was drawn with six or more sides and then the ends were ground off by hand to make a bead with 18 facets (see Chapter Seven, Czech Beads).

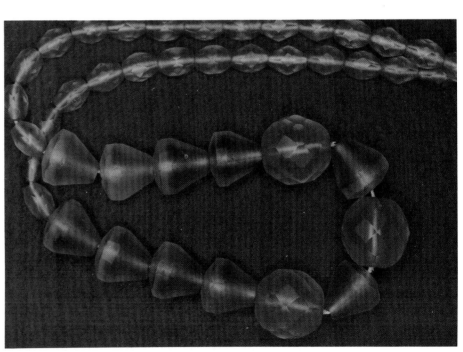

60 GLASS BEADS

GLASS BEAD COLORS

The colors of glass are made by putting various metal oxides into the batch. The color of the metal oxide has little to do with the color it produces because of the complex geography of the glass. When most glass is made it is a translucent green, produced by the universal presence of both the ferric and ferrous forms of iron. Cheap bottles are this color, and we call it "bottle-green."

To get rid of the green and make a clear glass, another ingredient is needed. Historically this was manganese, which forms a reddish-violet color. In the proper amounts it will cancel out the bottle-green and leave a clear glass, earning manganese the name "glassmakers' soap." Most clear glass today is made with selenium. However, it is difficult to get a pure clear glass; look at a windowpane on end and notice the slight green color.

With iron and copper a wide variety of glass colors are possible. In addition to the proper amount of ingredients, it is important to keep the furnace oxygenated (blowing air through it) or reduced (muffling or cutting off the air). These will produce different effects. In addition to iron, copper and manganese, the ancient glassmakers also commonly used cobalt for a deep blue and antimony, arsenic or tin to opacify the glass or make a white glass. For our interests, the newer glass ingredients are important because they can help us date beads in a collection. Some glass colors to look out for are:

Translucent (Ruby) Red Although the Chinese made a dusky version with copper for 1000 years, Europeans only discovered the more attractive gold version in the late 1600s. It was used sparingly except by the Bohemians until the 1800s, when Venice introduced white hearts, beads with a white opaque core and a translucent red coating. Around 1890 newly discovered selenium was employed, making a more garish ruby red. Venice abandoned it around 1930 because it was actually more expensive to use than gold. Both types can be mixed with white to make a pink color. Opaque selenium red is also common.

Opaque Yellows Most European bead yellows for the last several centuries were made by adding coal to the glass batch. The carbon would burn off and the sulfur would color the glass. Since this was difficult to measure exactly, the muted colors ended up in several hues, from canary to ocher. In the 1860s cadmium sulfide was introduced. This made a bright "Imperial" yellow, which is quite distinctive from the old, softer shades.

A very thin coating of metal will interrupt the transmission of light to give a rainbow or Aurora Borealis effect. An even thinner coating, as on the two pendants gives a Glacier Blue effect.

Yellow can be produced in several ways. The Venetian beads on top were colored by adding coal to the glass. Sulfur impurities give it the color, but it is difficult to measure, so a range of yellows and ochres result. The Venetian beads in the center were colored with cadmium sulphide, introduced around 1860. The Czech beads on the bottom are colored with uranium.

Red is a favorite color of many people, and red glass is always desired. On top are two ancient beads, the left one of translucent copper red from China the right one opaque red from India. The next two beads are translucent gold red. The next two are opaque red colored with selenium, and the tube at the bottom is translucent selenium red. Copper reds tend to be dull, gold reds rich and selenium reds garish.

Uranium Colors Uranium was discovered in Bohemia in the late 1700s and soon used in Czech (Bohemian) glass. It forms a variety of shades from a distinctive translucent yellow-green, to translucent and opaque yellow and orange. It is nearly always a marker for Czech beads, except that the Japanese use some uranium colors as well.

Goldstone or Aventurine Although not technically a color, this glass is very popular and fools many beginners. It is made by suspending tiny flakes of copper in a clear or transparent colored glass medium, in which they sparkle like gold. It was invented in the late 1600s in Venice, by accident (*per avventura*), it is said. It remained a Venetian monopoly until the mid-1800s, at which time it came to be used more and more as a decorative trailing on beads. Venice remains the major supplier today, but Bohemia and even China are known to have made it.

Black Glass Some authorities contend that there is no such thing as a true black glass. Without getting into an argument, it is correct that the bulk of black glass is not really black. When viewed against a strong light, especially if the glass is thin, it takes on a dark color, usually green or violet. The green is a result of a heavy concentration of iron and the violet of manganese. A very opaque black glass can also be made by adding organic material, such as goat dung, to the batch. Since these ingredients have been used for a long time, they are not chronological aids.

Goldstone or aventurine is created by tiny copper crystals suspended in translucent glass. It has traditionally been a Venetian art, but others learned to make it as well. Beads may be carved from chunks of the glass, or rods used to decorate beads, as on the black one. Perfect settling of the crystals is difficult, as the slab and large brown bead show with their dark lines.

Two strands worn by men in Peru. They consist of European trade beads, some of which are not known elsewhere, coins, crosses and natural objects. *Courtesy Joyce Griffiths.*

For much of the last five centuries, European wares have cornered the glass bead trade in most of the world. The reason for this is no mystery. Beginning in the late 1400s, Europeans began to explore and then conquer the globe. The wealth its colonies brought in, coupled with the Industrial Revolution, made Europe the unrivaled superpower for a long time.

From the start, European glass beads were introduced to the new regions Europeans encountered. Columbus handed them out on the very day he landed in the New World, "In order that they might develop a very friendly disposition toward us...." The European discoverers, explorers and settlers took glass beads with them, first as presents, then as items for barter, and finally as one of many commodities. While the old story of Manhattan being purchased for $24 worth of beads is a myth, much else was bought for beads: furs, land, gold and slaves.

VENICE: THE MOTHER OF MODERN BEADS

The opening of the Age of Exploration coincided with an important development in a small island in the lagoon of Venice. Then a great mercantile power, Venice was also a major glassmaking center. Many glassmakers were forced to move to the small island of Murano in 1291, as much to restrain them from taking their secrets elsewhere as to prevent the wooden buildings of the main city from catching fire.

Venice's commercial dealings already included a lively trade in pearl, ivory, rock crystal, bone and wooden beads. As the glass beadmakers skills improved, the crystal beadmakers sought to keep them in check and preserve their monopoly. However, around 1480 some Venetian beadmakers worked out an efficient system of making many beads at a time by drawing them (see Chapter Six). With the advantage of mass producing many glass beads of relatively uniform color and size, the crystal beadmakers were apprehensive. So successful were the glass beads just as Europeans were opening new markets around the globe, that by 1510 the ruling body of the Venetian guilds endorsed the glass beadmakers, forcing the rock crystal lobby into retreat.

Hence, the earliest European beads to flood the newly discovered worlds were Venetian drawn beads. In the 1500s and 1600s hardly any other sort of glass bead are found along the American Atlantic Coast or in West Africa. Eventually they dominated everywhere, though the process was slower in some places than in others.

A typical assortment of early 19th century Venetian lamp-wound beads. These popular trade beads were made into the last decades of the century.

A group of unusual Venetian trade beads, mostly of the early or mid 19th century. The disc bead at the bottom is highly decorated on the ends, as the example to its right shows. The green bead with aventurine is found principally in Egypt. Note the red bead with "37" on it; the other side is a poorly done example of the same number in Arabic numerals.

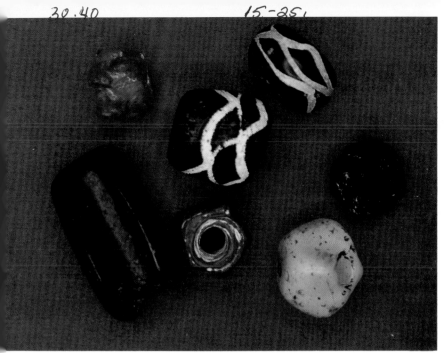

30.40   15-25

30.35   50-80

15.25

For a while there were successful Dutch rivals to Venice in Amsterdam and other Dutch cities. Their drawn beads can hardly be distinguished from contemporary Venetian beads. From roughly 1650 to 1750 they made more wound beads. The two blue beads have pentagonal sections. The white and black beads are called "twisted squares." The clear bead at the top is known as a "mulberry." The beads with wavy lines are very similar to some beads Venice made.

The Venetians did not sit on their laurels. They expanded and improved their products, and even by the early 1500s there were three beadmaking guilds. The Margariteri concentrated on plain drawn beads. The Paternosteri made drawn beads of more complexity, including chevrons. The Supialume made lamp-wound beads, though their apogee would come later. New effects were introduced: aventurine or goldstone, lattimo or milk glass, filigree glass and better and purer colors.

The most famous Venetian glassmakers of the early centuries were of the Miotti family. Antonio was making glass by 1542. Vincenzo was given the exclusive right to his invention of goldstone or aventurine in 1677. His brother Zuanne was famous for his milk glass. Both glass and beadmakers, the family continued in business until 1791.

THE ENVY OF EUROPE

The rest of Europe was jealous of Venice's near monopoly. For centuries kings and businessmen schemed to entice Venetian beadmakers away from the lagoon and into their own city or country. Some prominent beadmakers, including notably Zuan Antonio Miotti, were only too happy to oblige. France, Portugal, Spain, Holland, England, Austria and many Italian city-states played this game, some of them successful for a short time, but most of them coming to naught.

The earliest one of this group to thrive was Holland. Commencing in the late 1500s, bead factories were operating in Amsterdam and other Dutch cities. They produced a limited variety of mostly drawn beads, many duplicating Venetian ones, for a century. They also made some wound glass beads beginning late in the century, which sold well enough that the industry lasted until about 1750. Unfortunately for us, the bulk of the drawn beads were exactly like Venetian beads of the period, since many beadmakers or managers were from Venice. However, many of the wound beads have the advantage of being distinctive and easily recognized.

THE CZECH CHALLENGE

The greatest challenge to Venice, however, came from Bohemia, now in the Czech Republic. Before telling the story, a word about names. The people of Bohemia are Czechs, speak Czech and dominate the Czech Republic. They or their beads can be called Czech or Bohemian, but never "Czecho," a word that does not exist. Although some beads were made in Silesia across the border in Poland and in Moravia, the center has always been Jablonec nad Nisou (on the River Nisou), called Gablonz in German.

As at Venice, the story of Czech glass beads is rooted in stone working. The village of Turnov, like the capital of Prague, was a major center for cutting the bright red Bohemian garnets, known as pyrope. When the

Chevrons are the most popular beads of the last several centuries. The basic pattern has been given many variations which have not yet been dated or sourced. The two beads at top left have seven layers and are faceted; they date from ca. 1480-1580. The other two are typical of the 1600s. From that point on there was a great variety. The three beads in the fourth row may have been made in France. The one in the bottom row left might be Dutch; it and the three in the row above have been pinched into shape after reheating the tube. On bottom right is a Venetian bead made in the 1950s.

An early Czech technique was to mold a bead and then decorate it with ground lines. The lines in these beads have all been added with a grinding wheel.

Venetians began making translucent "ruby" red glass from gold following its invention in Germany, their cheap imitations depressed the market for genuine Bohemian garnets.

The garnet cutters of Turnov sent Wenceslas and Franz Fišer to Venice in 1706 to find work in glass factories and learn how the Venetians made red glass. After five years they returned, discouraged by the wall of secrecy they had encountered. But they must have learned something because by 1715 they had come up with a lead-based ruby red glass. The garnet cutters of Turnov began faceting this glass like garnets, but kept the work secret for much of the century. The Rybár family soon became the leaders in this new business, improving the glass, making canes and inventing a hand held mold for making blanks ready to facet. Shortly the mold was adapted for making beads.

In time, Turnov's secret leaked to surrounding villages. Many began making glass, often concentrating on imitation stones. Eventually, Jablonec nad Nisou became the center of this activity, which was spread throughout the Jizera (Iser in German) Mountains in Bohemia and adjacent territories. The first bead factory in Jablonec was opened in 1787 by Bernard Unger. At about the same time Jan Leopold Riedl, the founder of the leading beadmaking company in the area, began producing beads in his factories in neighboring towns. Much of the work was decentralized, with large glassmaking factories manufacturing canes or tubes that were later finished in small shops or homes throughout the region.

While the Czech beadmakers imitated some Venetian fashions, they also developed styles all their own. Some appealed to European tastes and were sold there, but early on they were doing a roaring business overseas. They developed new varieties to sell to specific markets in Africa, the Middle East and India. One secret of their success was the adaption of their stone grinding expertise on many of their glass beads either to decorate them or remove the seams from the molds used to form them. They also developed a system by which "sample men" roamed the globe, sometimes

Another popular Czech bead made with the help of grinding. These were drawn tubes with six sides, which were cut apart and had their twelve corners ground off. Such cornerless hexagonals were quite popular from about 1820 to 1900. Variations included different colors and longer beads with more facets.

The understanding of grinding processes served the Czech glass beadmakers well. These beads were made with a hand-held mold that left a conical perforation. They were then put on a stick and the facets ground on. As a group they are called "Vaseline" beads by American collectors after the common green color. Ca. 1830-1900.

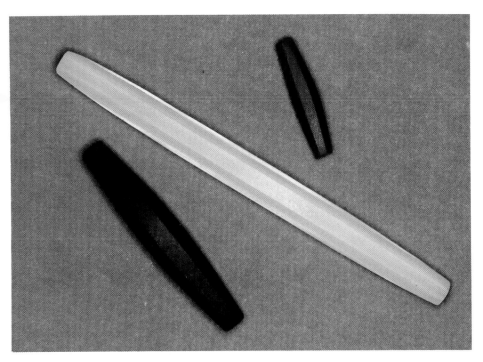

The Czechs made beads which were some-times quite spectacular. The brownish beads are carnelian imitations. The white bead has several layers of white and clear glass and is over 5 inches (130 cm) long. All were molded and then ground into octagonal barrels.

Czech beads typical of the end of the 19th century. The pendant with the flower design might be from a few decades later. The square cylinder at lower left was wound and pressed with a design; the other beads are molded.

for two years, visiting remote corners of Asia, Africa and America. These men would buy a few of the most valued beads they encountered to send home, where the beads would be imitated in glass, no matter what their original material.

Bohemian business boomed. Jablonec grew into a city, had a steamship named after it and became an early railroad terminus. By the 1860s the Bohemians were outselling the Venetians. Venice had gone through a long stage of decline, linked to the political fortunes of the once mighty empire, now reduced to a province of a unified Italy. If Venetian beadmaking were to survive, some changes had to be made.

NEW ACTIVITIES AND DECLINE

The 1860s was a period of intense activity among Venetian beadmakers, at least in part due to Czech competition. During that time, several new machines, processes and glasses were introduced, some of them improvements of older inventions. One result was a much greater uniformity in the sizes and colors of small drawn "seed beads," which had become so important in beadwork worldwide. Another was a wider variety of lamp-wound beads, which had come into their own by the 1800s.

The Czechs found a large and ready market in the Islamic world and geared production to it. Crescents and star motifs were popular. The middle round bead says "Mohammed." The violet colored bead has the opening line to the chapters of the Qoran. The red pendant is a degenerate Talhakimt, originally made in carnelian. The round beads are still in production; the others are older, with the violet bead being early 19th century.

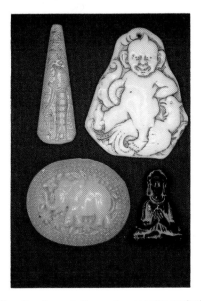

One Czech speciality was to appeal to particular markets or make beads of novelty designs. The yellow Egyptian pendant, an earring, was made after Tutakhnantan's tomb was opened in the 1920s. The elephant bead was apparently to wear on the upper arm, probably for the Indian market, though bought in Egypt. The blue Buddha and large troll probably had wider markets.

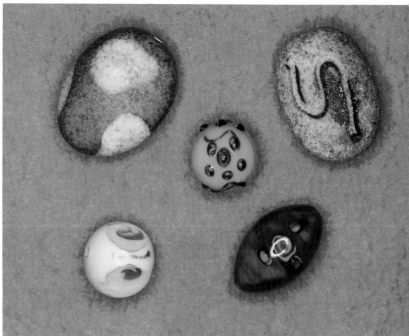

Some Czech beads of the late 1980s and early 1990s. As markets changed, so did designs of beads in newly liberated Bohemia. All these beads are lamp-wound.

Czech beads of the late 20th century. All are molded, and nearly all would fit into any decorative design. The dice bead is, ironically, popular as a worry bead among Muslims, who are adverse to gambling.

Another niche exploited by the Czechs was to imitate other people's beads and materials. At far right are three small turquoise imitations, often called "Hubble beads" in the American trade. To their left is a yellow bead imitating African powder-glass beads made in a horizontal mold. To its left is a large black "French jet" bead. The long white bead imitates shell for the northeast Indian market. To its left are imitations of lapis lazuli, onyx, coral and granite, popular in West Africa. To the right of the long bead is a tortoise shell imitation and a genuine and imitation Arca shell bead, valued in Nigeria.

At the end of the 1800s and the beginning of the 1900s both Venice and Bohemia had to adjust to new realities. In Venice increased rivalry from other centers led to a consolidation of 17 beadmaking houses into the Societa' Veneziana per l'Industria della Conterie in 1898 (*conterie* refers to seed beads). While this strengthened the Venetians' hand, the two World Wars and the Depression weakened the business. Following decolonization, even more competitors were born (see Chapters Eight through Eleven). Most intense was the Japanese threat, which forced the Conterie out of business in 1985. Venice was no longer making "seed beads."

Lamp-wound beads became a crucial part of Venetian production. Beautiful hand crafted beads made from interesting glasses with spectacular decorations were the hallmark of such famous masters as Giovanni Giacomuzzi, Lorenzo Radi, Antonio Salviati and Dominico Bussolin, who initiated the change from oil to gas lamps for the work. Jacobo Franchini and his son Giovan were celebrated for their intricate mosaic canes, including realistic portraits. By the end of the century, millefiori beads had become an important item.

Venetian lamp-wound beads made at the end of the 19th century and early in the 20th.

Venetian lamp-wound beads typical of the late 19th century after improvements were made to the lamp for winding, the glasses and the designs. Combed designs were especially popular.

Venetian beads of the 1920s and 1930s. Note the cadmium sulfide yellow and selenium reds. Floral designs were not as well done as several decades before.

Venetian lamp-wound floral decorated beads of about 1880-1920. These were produced especially for European and American ladies rather than for the African market.

Some unusual Venetian millefiori beads. The design on the bead in center bottom is a crude rooster, symbol of Murano Island, Venice. The two beads at bottom right are decorated with canes laid along their length and then others placed on their sides. Most cores are black or cobalt blue, not red. The oval millefiori at bottom left is scarce. At top right is a bead with a wave decoration further decorated with mosaic chips.

Special Venetian millefiori beads include "elbows" or curved tubes and beads flattened into tabular shapes.

Venetian beads of recent manufacture. The top two beads were made in the 1950s, the others in the 1970s and 1980s. Work is not as elaborate as earlier, though with higher prices this is beginning to change again.

In Bohemia, by 1904 a decision was made to concentrate production on beads with a universal appeal and less for specific markets, which had perhaps been satiated by that time. The turbulent events of the first half of the century also diminished markets, but Czechoslovakia fell into an even greater danger as it became Communist after World War II. Nationalization quickly followed, and beadmaking was moribund for a decade until the new regime recognized its export potential. Just as debilitating was a massive exodus (expulsion) of Czech beadmakers to the western side of the Iron Curtain.

BEADMAKERS ELSEWHERE IN EUROPE

Despite the leadership of Venice and Bohemia in glass beadmaking, other European nations produced them as well. Britain was never a major bead power, though some were made there. Perhaps the most interesting were small beads wound by itinerant tinkerers for women to tie onto their lace bobbins. Except for the modern imitation pearl industry, Spain made few beads, even though the first small wound green and yellow beads Columbus and early Spaniards handed out were local products. Russia, Belgium and a few other countries are known to have made glass beads, but aside from Holland, only France, Germany and Austria stand out as important secondary producers.

By 1904 the Bohemians decided not to gear their production so heavily into beads meant for small niche markets and to produce those to appeal to a wider audience. These Art Nouveau and Art Deco beads of the early 20th century were skillfully molded and ground to remove seams along the edges.

The principal makers of glass beads in England were tinkers who made them for lace bobbins. Recently the art has been revived, making beads to resemble the old ones. The small square beads are called "square cuts," but are actually just paddled into shape.

France

France was making beads by the late 1400s and a guild was established in 1569. In the 1600s they were exporting beads, some to England. Around 1656 a Parisian beadmaker named Jacquin perfected an imitation pearl, which became widely popular. Men drew thin tubes of clear glass and women inflated these over a lamp, then poured in the pearly protein guanine, extracted from the scales of the alewife fish, to coat the inside. They then added wax to protect the guanine and give the bead heft, and finally the beads were perforated with a piece of rolled up paper, the fibers of which would cling to the wax to prevent the thread from getting sticky. Few of these "Roman pearls" retain their original appeal; the industry closed early in this century.

In the 1700s there was a craze in France for jewelry to mourn the dead. French beadmakers made black glass beads, which came to be called

French fashion has dictated many sorts of beads. Around Lyons a few companies make drawn beads. Though today mostly monochromes or white hearts, striped beads and chevrons were produced in the 1930s. The bead shaped like a flower was made by René Lalique. The string on the left is of cut steel and on the right aluminum, both now out of production.

For much of this century the firm of Pierre Rousselet in Paris has been one of the leading fashion beadmakers of Europe. The lamp-wound beads are often striking in their free-form shapes.

Wound annulars or rings made in Germany during the last century. Before about 1850 the blues had a gray tint, as the bead in the center. Amber was the only other color at that time. Clear ones came in by 1860, and by the end of the century the blues had bright cobalt shades and green ones appeared. Production stopped about 1900.

"French jet." Thus, the fashion began in France long before Victoria was mourning Albert in England. Most later "French jet" was made in Bohemia.

In 1864 J. Felix Bapterosses in Braire began making beads with the Prosser machines designed for buttons. He improved the machines and added some milk to the mixture, and his bead business grew considerably. Although Holland, Austria and Germany also made these beads, only the French rivaled the Czechs in volume.

By the late 1900s beadmakers using the drawing method made small "seed" beads, commonly called rocailles, around Lyons in the south. They were connected with Venetian firms. An independent house was started in 1929 by two Venetians and this and another house survive. The French make a fairly large proportion of drawn beads, chevrons with few layers and "seed" beads.

The early 1900s saw the establishment or growth of houses making lamp-wound beads for the fashion industry. Many were located around Paris, and a few survive to this day. The best known was that of René Lalique, though beads and jewelry were only part of his output. The largest was owned by Pierre Rousselet, who had 800 workers in the 1920s and produced casein plastic beads and imitation pearls as well. Société Alex and Masion Gripoix are still operating, producing fine beads on special order.

Germany and Austria

In the area of present-day Germany, beads were being made by the end of the 1200s from Venetian glass. In the late 1500s glassmaking had begun at Lauscha in the Thuringia Forest. By the early 1800s a speciality developed there of making blown beads which were silvered inside. The Czechs also made such beads, and eventually drove the Thuringians out of business. Other beadmaking centers included Potsdam, Saxony (which made an inferior false pearl), and perhaps Nuremburg.

The major center developed in the Royal Forest around the town of Warmensteinach. Venetians taught the locals there in 1486 how to make black wound rosary beads using the local "beadstone" (a type of hornblende) as the basic raw material. From the 1700s to the late 1800s this was a major beadmaking area, and their beads were exported widely, though little is yet known of this early production. Beadmaking stopped with World War II, though a small jewelry industry remains, using old stocks of beads.

Beads made in Warmensteinach, Germany. The two wound beads on the upper left are from the 1920s. The others are molded beads made soon after World War II following an influx of Czech beadmakers, who later moved to Neu Gablonz.

Austria does not seem to have been a center for beads early on, but by 1814 Bohemia was part of the Austro-Hungarian Empire. A young inventive Bohemian beadmaker, Daniel Swarovski, developed a way to mechanically facet beads and rhinestones of high quality. Worried that other Jablonec beadmakers would copy his machines, he moved to the tiny village of Wattens, near Innsbruck, in 1895. There he continued inventing new devices for cutting beads, began making his own glass, and in time expanded into producing grinding wheels, fine cut crystal, optics and other related products. Austrian cut crystal beads, among the most popular and stylish on the world market, are made by the Swarovski firm, with factories around the world doing a billion-dollar-a-year business.

However, today many beadmakers in both Germany and Austria are relatively new because they left Bohemia when Communism took over in the middle of this century. In Germany they first went to Warmensteinach and Gmünd, a major jewelry center, but eventually (after 1945) moved to the southern town of Kaufbeuren, where they established themselves in a suburb named Neu Gablonz (New Jablonec). They were aided in their settlement by the earlier immigrant, Daniel Swarovski, who opened his first foreign sales office there. Others went to various localities in Austria, including Krimsmünster and Vienna. One Viennese beadmaking company also calls itself Neu Gablonz.

Cut crystal beads of the Daniel Swarovski Corp. of Wattens, Austria. The compartmented box is the way these beads are packed. Shown here is a variety of sizes, colors and finishes of a single bead style.

Glass beads made in Germany shortly after World War II. The small black beads come with a tag saying they were made in the U.S. Zone; the other two strands have tags saying Western Germany.

Beads from Neu Gablonz, Germany, 1980s. Many are similar to Czech beads, because the beadmakers came from there after World War II. All are molded, including the two small round ones at bottom center, made to look as though they were wound.

After World War II some refugees from Czechoslovakia settled at Krimsmünster, Austria. Bead production there resembles Czech molded beads, but the oval beads with decorative holes are apparently unique to this center. The bead at top right has been molded but not finished; note the flash which seeped out between the halves of the mold.

Austria also has refugee beadmakers living in and around Vienna. These beads were produced by a company called Neu Gablonez (New Jablonec), just like the German town of beadmakers. All beads are molded, including the "cut" faceted ones.

This large region of the world is home to innumerable bead enterprises, major and minor. Four of the six great global industries are located here, as are many smaller ones. The Middle East is a largely Muslim territory that stretches from Morocco on the Atlantic Ocean through North Africa and the Arabian Peninsula, north to Turkey and on east to Iran, Afghanistan and Pakistan. India as we use it here means the Indian subcontinent, including Pakistan, India, Bangladesh and smaller countries like Nepal and Sri Lanka. We begin with a short history of ancient beadmaking here and then look at more recent industries.

ANCIENT BEADMAKING

Glass in the Middle East

Glass was invented in the Middle East in what is now Iraq or the area to the north some 4500 years ago. Beads were the first glass product, and beadmaking spread to many centers, most notably along the eastern end of the Mediterranean in what are now Syria, Lebanon and Israel. By Classical times, the industry was in full swing. Glass beads were made here by several different processes, some of which have not survived to our day. A major beadmaking center was the new city of Alexandria, Egypt, where some of the finest and most expensive beads are believed to have been made. The beads of this industry were traded long distances, though probably not in great number; some reached China and even Korea.

Beadmaking continued through the declining years of the Roman Empire and into the period when this region swiftly adapted Islam. During the seventh to twelfth centuries many of the same beads were made as had been produced earlier. The Muslim world traded actively with Africa and Asia, and their beads are found in fairly large numbers in cities with which they had close contact.

India is a land of beads. Left: a strand of hard Rudraksha (Siva's eye) seeds worn by followers of Lord Siva. They are usually divided into five segments; the single bead is a less common three-faceted one; below it is a seed of a related species. Center is a strand of small shell beads strung with some green glass beads in Rameswarum, Tamil Nadu, a city holy to Lord Rama. Right, a string of Purdalpur glass beads, metal spacers and a bell to put on cattle for protection and identification, bought in a village market.

Beads made around Damascus, Syria in the 1970s and 80s. Their designs and matte finish make them look like ancient Middle Eastern beads. However, they were made by binding glass particles with a plastic, apparently in an attempt to fool would-be buyers.

Because of the ethnic and religious mixture of India, beads made in Purdalpur are destined for many markets. Those on the top row, including the dZi imitation, are decorated with powdered glass. The blue heart has an "Aum," sacred to Hindus and the clear heart says "Allah." The red and black bead has a figure of Hanuman, the monkey who helped save Rama. The small beads at bottom center are made by one master by adding each tiny ground glass ball separately to the central tube.

From the eleventh through the fifteenth centuries Christian Crusaders and Asian Mongols swept through the Islamic world. The constant wars and raids destroyed many glassmaking cities, at least some of which we know made beads: Tyre and Sidon, Fustat (Old Cairo) and Damascus and Aleppo.

Some of the beadmakers were taken away. For example, Timur transplanted Damascus beadmakers to his capital at Samarkand. Others, perhaps chiefly from Tyre, went to live and work in Hebron, one of the oldest cities in the world, near Jerusalem. But the industry was badly hurt and never regained its old glory.

Beadmaking in India

In India, stone beadmaking dates back even further than glass beadmaking in the Middle East. The Indus Valley or Harappan Civilization was centered in modern Pakistan, but controlled territory into Afghanistan and far into India. Its people had a genius for making and decorating different sorts of stone beads. Many of these were exported to ancient Mesopotamia (Iraq), while others were used locally. There were beadmakers in several Harappan cities, one of which, Lothal, is near the world's best known carnelian and agate/onyx deposits at Ratanpur.

Beadmaking continued in India after the breakup of the Harappans, and joined the international scene again when Rome began active trading with the subcontinent. The ports of western India were visited to buy beads made from Ratanpur stones cut in and around the great inland city of Ujjain. The suspension of Roman trading did not stop the beadmaking industry; it remained the major source of stone beads all around the Indian Ocean, into Europe and the African interior and throughout Asia.

The Romans also traded with south India. There stone beads were available that were not found in Ratanpur. These included beryl (related to emerald), pearls, garnets, quartz crystal and amethyst. This industry was inventive and learned to make citrine from amethyst and black onyx from agate.

A leading export at this time was not strictly a bead, but blanks of onyx into which cameos could be carved. First and second century Romans were crazy about cameos: the red and white or brown and white sardonyx came from Ratanpur, while the black and white onyx came from the great southeastern port we know today as Arikamedu.

Imported European beads are used for beadwork in many parts of the Middle East. These are mostly older pieces made in Afghanistan. At top is a triangular charm case and a large triangular piece which decorates cattle. At bottom is a man's pouch, a bangle and a roundel used for women's clothing. Note the wear on the beads in the bangle.

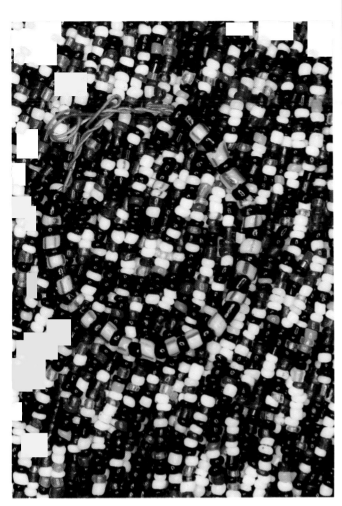

Black wound glass beads with white eyes are produced today in Uzbekistan, probably in or near Tashkent. The beadmakers may be related to the family which moved to Afghanistan in 1917.

The drawn beads of Papanaidupet, India are made in the same unique way employed for Indo-Pacific beads in south India for 2200 years or more. The modern beads are composed of better quality glass. On the hank is a child's bracelet strung on a wire and bought in a village in the north.

Arikamedu was also home to a major glass bead industry. The Indians invented a complex but serviceable way to draw a large number of glass tubes, unlike the method described in Chapter Six. A team of a dozen men worked up to 100 pounds (40 to 50 kgs) of glass into a large cone, which was held on a long iron tube called a *lada*. A rod was inserted into the tube and used to smash a hollow center through the cone. The whole was returned to the furnace and on the other side a master reached in with a hook to secure a continuous tube being pulled off the tip of the rod. He then pulled the tubing out hand-over-hand, a process taking up to three hours. The tubes were cut apart and heated in ash to form small monochrome glass beads. These Indo-Pacific beads, as they are called, are the most common beads of the ancient world and found from Mali to Bali, Ghana to China and South Africa to South Korea for 2000 years.

From Arikamedu, beadmakers fanned out to other cities in Asia. In the first century or so they went to Mantai, Sri Lanka (Ceylon) and two cities of Funan, the first state in Southeast Asia, one now in Vietnam and one in Thailand. As the Funan Kingdom broke up, the beadmakers came under the sway of the Sumatran based kingdom of Srivijaya, making beads at the capital of the same name and at two places in Malaysia and one in Thailand. When Srivijaya declined, so did Indo-Pacific beads in Southeast Asia. The Indian industry continued at Arikamedu itself, moving to the only place where these beads are still made, the village of Papanaidupet in southern India probably in the 1600s.

Simple wound beads in amber, blue, green and clear glass were made by a family in Herat, Afghanistan during much of the century. They left their home in Bokhara, Uzbekistan in 1917 when Communism came in. Herat was badly damaged by the civil war in the 1980s and beadmaking has probably ceased there. The two bright beads on top were made in Bokhara before 1917.

Beads made in Hebron before about 1880 from Dead Sea salts. They are opaque in limited colors. Some green ones were paddled to make a cornerless cube. The only decorated one known from this time is the black bead with the crumb decoration. These beads were popular in the eastern Sudan, in what are now Sudan and Chad and on to the west coast of Africa.

RECENT BEADMAKING

Beadmakers in the Middle East and India work in materials ranging from gold and silver to wood and clay. There are many industries, some large, some small, throughout this region. It should be remembered that in India this work has long been based on caste, and there are specific beadmaking castes. Though this ancient system is breaking down in some places, it remains a strong force. We cannot possibly cover all bead industries in this region, but shall look at the major ones and some of the more interesting minor ones.

Middle Eastern Glass

Following the destruction of glassmaking and beadmaking centers in the Middle East during the Middle Ages, the glass bead industry was split into two parts. One consisted of prisoners taken to Central Asia, where they either set up new shops or joined glassmaking shops already established. There is still a small industry in Uzbekistan, but nothing is known of it yet.

One family of glassmakers from this branch left Uzbekistan in 1917 when Communism took over the former Soviet Union. Good Muslims, they could not stand the new atheistic doctrines, and so moved from Bokhara to Herat, Afghanistan. There they made simple, monochrome glass beads in clear, amber, blue and green colors by the furnace-winding method. What happened to them during the more recent years of fighting that devastated Herat is not known.

The other branch of beadmakers apparently emigrated from Tyre on the Mediterranean coast to Hebron near Jerusalem sometime after the twelfth century. They made beads there, using the salts of the Dead Sea as their alkali. Their glass was opaque yellow and green, sometimes blue and black. The beads were furnace-wound and were popular in Egypt and in sub-Saharan Africa. Around 1880 or so, they stopped making their own glass and began melting down broken bottles, which were becoming more available. This brighter glass they made into beads and amulets, including one featuring a stratified eye for warding off the Evil Eye. By the middle of this century their inventory had become simpler and they were no longer making the Evil Eye beads.

About a century ago a pair of brothers left Hebron and emigrated to western Turkey, as both places were part of the Ottoman Empire, which encouraged the spread of craft techniques. They began making simple

Current production of beads in Hebron is quite simple. Only a small range of colors and shapes are used for beads furnace-wound from remelted glass.

blue beads for animals in Izmir and probably also introduced the Evil Eye bead at this time. Around 1930 they were forced to abandon their workshops by their neighbors, who were tired of the smoke and afraid of the danger of fire. They settled in the village of Gorece. About 1960 Zakai Erdal introduced changes in their designs, many of them inspired by ancient Roman beads he saw in the numerous museums of ancient cities nearby. For personal reasons, a few beadmakers set out on their own in the next decade and opened shops at Kemalpasa and Bodrum, Turkey.

One other bead industry traces its roots to Hebron. A glassmaker from Cairo, which had ceased making beads for centuries, went to live in Hebron in the 1930s. There he married a local girl and learned beadmaking from his father-in-law. This he carried back to Cairo to reestablish beadmaking in the old center.

Middle Eastern Faience

Even before the rise of glass beads, faience dominated beadmaking in the Middle East and far beyond. Faience has a core of quartz grains which are not completely melted, but stick together at their edges. Over that is a glaze, a thin layer of true glass. Faience beads were once very popular in much of the Old World. Only two places survive that make it today, and both start with the letter "Q."

One is the holy city of Qom, Iran. Local quartz stones are ground up and mixed with fine clay and frit. Beads are hand-rolled into shape by children and then drilled by other youngsters. The beads are packed in a crucible with soda and copper for coloring and then fired. When done, they emerge as relatively spherical bright blue beads. These are not worn by people, but tied onto animals for protection against the Evil Eye; they are popularly called "donkey beads," and are the remnants of an ancient industry.

The other is in Egypt, a village across the Nile from Luxor called Qorna. As it is near the Valley of the Kings, Qorna was once the home of many tomb robbers. When the local officials brutally put an end to that practice, the people of Qorna took to imitating the goods they once found in the tombs. The beads they make are of steatite. Some, such as scarabs, are carved from a small block of steatite and glazed and fired. Simple faience beads are made from steatite paste rolled around a straw and heated in the sun. Then a glaze or color is sprinkled on and the beads are fired together with dung as the fuel. Some of these beads look very much like ancient Egyptian faience, except that they are composed of soapstone, not quartz, and are completely opaque.

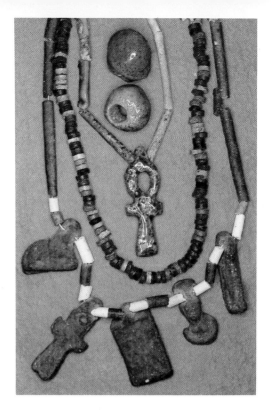

Modern faience beads made in the Middle East. The two round beads at top were made in Qom, Iran and used to keep the Evil Eye away from animals. Strands made in Qorna, Egypt are sold to tourists. They are unlike the Qom faience or ancient faience, as they are made of soapstone, not quartz. The matte look is favored because it resembles ancient faience.

Other Middle Eastern Beads

The variety of beads made in the Middle East is astonishing. Nearly all of them are for local consumption, as they are so often used for amuletic and other special purposes. Among these are beads with a sweet scent, since the people are so fond of perfumes. In addition to the scented paste beads mentioned in Chapter Four, cloves are widely worn by brides, especially in Arabia and around the Persian Gulf.

From the days of the Prophet Mohammed, Muslim men have been enjoined not to wear gold, though silver is acceptable. Women are allowed to wear gold, but silver is also very popular with them; they wear both metals for ornament, charms and as a portable bank account. Many silver pieces are meant to keep away the Evil Eye; not only their shapes do this, but so does the metal itself.

A popular charm is made in the form of a small case. Into this case is placed a paper which has been written by a holy man with either a short verse of the Qoran or a magical number square. Other auspicious objects may also be included. The cases are made from leather in some instances, but metals are also very popular. The shape of the case has been duplicated by imitations in stone, particularly from western India, and glass, especially Czech.

Islamic tradition is strongly against men wearing gold, but silver is acceptable and has the advantage of being powerful against the Evil Eye. Silver filigree beads are found in many parts of the Middle East, here from Iran. The one in the center is modern; the others much older; note the wear on several of them.

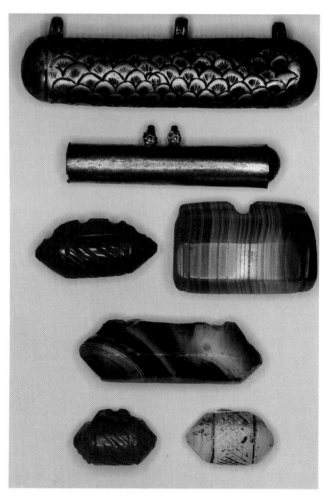

Elongated charm cases of metal hold holy phrases or magical squares; the silver one is from Iran and the copper one from India. The shape has been duplicated in stone, here in red jasper, agate and carnelian from India. On bottom right is a Czech glass imitation.

Indian Glass Beads

Up until the last century there were dozens of villages in India where glass beads and bangles (a very important Indian accessory, usually made by beadmakers) were produced. The British ruined this local industry, first by insisting that Indians buy British made or British imported goods. As this began to impoverish India, the colonists embarked on an industrialization policy which concentrated production in large European-owned factories. Village-based industries, the age-old backbone of Indian wealth, were thus destroyed. It happened to glass beads as well as steel, cloth and every other industry.

Today there are only a few glass bead centers in India and Pakistan. Firozabad has been built up into the glass capital of India, making most decorative glass in the country. It also produces the bulk of bangles. The only beads made there are hollow blown ones, silvered inside, a technique taught them a couple of decades ago by some Japanese. Recently glass beadmaking has also been introduced in Bombay.

Benaras (Varanasi) has long been a bead producer. It has been making ivory beads for ages: there is reference to the craft 1000 years ago. It is also the center for drilling Rudraksha seeds, and produces wooden and stone beads. In villages around the city women string beads into finished pieces and make strands with each bead on an individual wire link. In 1942 a Czech couple went to Benaras to teach the locals how to make glass. A school was established, and though that has since closed and glassmaking no longer goes on, Benaras has a thriving glass bead industry. They make lamp-wound beads in ever increasing varieties, and have even begun to imitate some old Venetian beads.

Blown beads from Firozabad, India. At top is a tube to be heated and shaped in a long mold. Tubes of beads are then filled with silver ammonia nitrite to leave a silvery coat inside. If the tube is amber colored, the beads will be golden; if clear, they will be silver. Other colors can also be used.

Benaras, India became a major glass beadmaking center after Czechs taught the rudiments of lamp-working in the 1940s. These are beads typically found in Indian markets. The dark blue ones connected with wires are shaped like the sacred conch.

India has more recently boomed as an exporter. Many designs have been suggested by Western buyers and resemble old Venetian beads. The goldstone is imported from Venice; the other glasses made in Firozabad.

A traditional beadmaking center is Purdalpur, near Agra. The north Indian glass beadmakers' caste was converted to Islam around 1700. When India and Pakistan split in 1947, about half the beadmakers went to Pakistan, where the government set up commercial glass factories and allowed the refugees to operate small furnaces in and around Hyderabad. The beads they make are similar to those made in India. Those who chose to stay in India left their various villages and concentrated in Purdalpur, where there are now several dozen furnaces and many different beadmaking styles being practiced.

Purdalpur beads are nearly all furnace wound (though beadmakers trained in Benaras also do lamp-winding). Some styles made can be dated back 1500 years or more. Others are more recent, including the Indian version of millefiori beads. Though older beadmakers know how to make glass, and did until recently, most of their glass now comes from Firozabad. Because there is such a variety of beadmakers, each one working their own styles in one village, there is a great assortment of beads coming from Purdalpur.

In south India is the remnant of the Indo-Pacific bead industry, discussed above. The beadmakers appear to have settled in Papanaidupet in the 1600s. They still make drawn beads the old way, but the beads look different from ancient Indo-Pacific beads because the glass quality is better. They use glass both bought from Firozabad and some made locally.

Purdalpur has a long glass beadmaking tradition and became home to many beadmakers from north India after Independence in 1947. The variety of beads made there is astounding; each household has its own speciality. The two long tubes are drawn; the other beads are furnace-wound. The white bead with the flower at lower left has been painted with a stencil.

Millefiori beads from Purdalpur. As Venetian millefiories become increasingly expensive, these grow in popularity. At the bottom is a piece of a fancy drawn cane. Note the face beads and face cane section in the center.

Because north Indian glass beadmakers were Muslims, about half emigrated to Pakistan after Independence. They were settled in Hyderabad and make beads which often resemble Indian work. The Pakistanis, however, tend to use more swirled glass than the Indians.

Indian Stone Beadmaking

The Indian stone bead industry has not changed much for many centuries, except that it has become ever more concentrated in the city of Cambay (Khambat). Today raw materials are shipped to Cambay from all over India and even abroad. The once very tight hold that caste had on the industry has been loosened somewhat, but the shop owners who control the process are still at the top of the pecking order, while the Bhil tribals who dig the stones at Ratanpur are at the bottom (lucky to get fifty cents a day for the whole working family). Some mechanization has crept in, but many of the old processes continue (See Chapter Five).

The skill of Indian lapidaries has been translated into a program to train Indians to cut diamonds. Today more diamonds are cut in India than in any other country in the world, though the stones they work are small. The diamond cutters are often of the Patel caste of farmers; many stone beadmakers are also Patels. Jaipur has begun to rival Cambay as a stone beadmaking center recently. Jaipur has long been a key manufacturer of jewelry, and more recently has been making stone beads, often small tumbled chips drilled by ultrasound. The government of the southern state of Tamil Nadu has plans to revive its ancient stone bead industry.

Other Indian Beads

India is literally a land of beads, where almost any material is made into beads by someone. There is a rule of thumb to be followed when looking for beads in the country: they are most often sold where people congregate, such as places of pilgrimage and tourist spots. It is hard to find a bead shop just anywhere, but visit the Ajunta caves, the Taj Mahal, Madras' Marine Beach or a holy place, and you will find bead stalls. Since the sellers of beads are members of the same caste as the beadmakers, we often find beadmakers in these cities, too.

We have already noted how many kinds of beads are made in Benaras, the most holy of cities. Rameswarum in the far south, sacred to Lord Rama, is home to the major shell bead industry of the country. Shells are strung into beads at many other resort places, too, including Pondicherry and Kanniyakumari.

Puri is a sacred city for the Jaganath cult. Beadmakers there dye reeds, cut them into fragile tubes and string them. Others cut beads and elaborate crowns from sola pith, and still others make beads for weddings. These latter were once made of camphor. Four hours in a hot and lively wedding party meant that the beads would disappear, as the camphor sublimated (turned from a solid to a gas). The beadmakers will still make camphor beads on request, but nowadays use their little two-part molds mostly to form similar but much longer lasting *malas* (garlands) from paraffin.

The story goes on an on; it could fill a whole book by itself. Indian beads are cut from wood in many places, especially from the holy basil and sweet-smelling sandal. Silk cocoons and silk strands are made into garlands. Lac, the product of an insect and the basis of shellac, is used both to color wooden beads and other items and also as a base for beads or bangles themselves. There is a man in Tanjor locally famous for his wedding garlands made of rice grains individually sewed into trimmings and decorated with beads of cloves, mace, nutmeg and pressed sandalwood powder. And, of course, there are silver and gold jewelers and beadmakers everywhere.

Cambay (Khambat), Gujarat is the center for stone beadmaking in India. The carnelians come from nearby Ratanpur, but other stones, including the blue sodalite and the white colored agates come from other locales.

And more Indian beads. Top left: two strands of dyed reeds from Puri, Orissa. Fragile and cheap, they are worn by girls. Bottom left: a pendant of lac decorated with beads, wire and mirrors for export. Center: a garland of molded paraffin beads made in Puri as a wedding necklace, which have largely replaced camphor beads because the latter is much more expensive and transient. Right: string of castor oil plant seeds from Benaras.

CHAPTER NINE
FAR EAST

24. - 40. 5t.

Strands of Chinese beads imported into the U.S. about 1920. These are typical of beads made for export at that time, colorful but not too finely crafted.

Eastern Asia is dominated historically and culturally by China, though the reality is by no means as monolithic as we might at first believe. China itself is home to many different people and was united only at certain times during its history. The modern countries of Korea and Japan have been deeply influenced by China, but are societies with traditions peculiarly their own.

The story of Chinese beads, particularly glass beads, is not as well known as some others. For a long time it was believed that China did not make or export glass beads to any extent. It has been noted that the Chinese got along well without glass, using oiled paper for windows, ceramics for vessels and jade for ornaments. It was also assumed that glass was relatively new to China and introduced from the outside. We now know differently.

As for Korea and Japan, many outsiders see them as adjuncts to China. This is not true, as each has maintained its own culture for thousands of years, despite the proximity of the Middle Kingdom. Their bead story is quite different from China's, as are many of their customs.

BACKGROUND OF THE CHINESE BEAD TRADE

The oldest glass beads found in China are some 3000 years in age. The glass is distinctive, as it is heavy in both lead and barium, the latter virtually unknown in any other ancient glass. The Chinese probably invented glass as an off-shoot to their metal production and used lead from one or more mines that had a lot of barium in the ore or they may have introduced the barium to give the glass a jade-like opacity. After the Han period (ending in A.D. 200), barium is no longer found, but lead continued to be a hallmark of Chinese beads.

The Chinese used glass beads themselves to imitate precious stones, especially the "Stone of Heaven" as they called jade. Jade imitations are found from the beginning of Chinese glass beadmaking, and many jade items in museums and private collections are actually glass. We do not yet know much about the export of Chinese beads early in their history, though some went to Korea and Japan. It seems likely that much of it was destined for the "Western Barbarians," the nomads of Central Asia, whom the Chinese were always trying to pacify.

The 1100s were a crossroads in Chinese history. The Mongols of the north moved south, capturing everything in their way. The Chinese were displaced, and half the population eventually resettled in the six small, mountainous provinces of the southern seaboard. The Song dynasty relocated its capital near the sea and took a great interest in maritime trade, building the world's first permanent navy and adapting many new nautical inventions. Commerce was especially directed toward Southeast Asia, and from this date the countries of that region were inundated with Chinese glass beads, which gives us an excellent idea of what they were like.

After the Mongols captured all of China in 1279 they, surprisingly, took to the sea themselves, and even waged war against Japan (through thrown back by a typhoon) and Java in Indonesia. They continued to trade the beads made in the swollen, industrialized cities of the south. The Ming, who restored Chinese domination in the late 1300s, sent out enormous fleets on no less than seven expeditions; the largest one had 62 large ships with some 37,000 soldiers. They visited as far away as Africa and brought a giraffe home that they regarded as the celestial sign of a unicorn. But the Ming decided that there was nothing China needed from the rest of the world, and turned their backs on it.

What are thought of as "typical" Chinese glass beads are not too well formed, often have large holes and are of bubbly glass. Most telling is the range of colors the Chinese developed under Imperial patronage. Late 19th-early 20th century.

A Chinese form of mosaic decoration was apparently achieved by rolling up a clear glass plate with stripes. When sliced, a starburst pattern was formed which was used to decorate beads. The bead in the center is better made and likely older than the others.

Yet beads continued to be traded in Southeast Asia and in time further afield. In order to outflank Portugal, the Spanish set up a trans-Pacific link between Acapulco, Mexico and Manila in the Philippines. Every year great galleons loaded with Mexican and Bolivian silver would land at Manila, where the silver would buy the luxuries of the East from Indian, Thai, Korean, Japanese, Cambodian and especially Chinese traders. These were sent back to Acapulco, where the fine silks and porcelains were taken across to Veracruz and sent to Seville. The cheaper goods, including Indian carnelians and Chinese glass beads, remained in the Americas.

Somewhat later, the Russians confirmed that there was a great land east of Siberia. From the first voyage of the Dane Vitus Bering, the Russians were giving Chinese beads away to the people they met in Alaska. The Russians could not dock at Chinese ports, and were forced to buy beads from the Chinese at the one approved outpost on the Mongolian border; beads were one of the few goods charged no duty. Chinese beads were later imported by the British and Yankees, and the Russians also brought beads from Europe and even made some of their own.

This short summary should convince you that Chinese glass beads have an old history and have been important trade items for a long time. This comes as something of a surprise to many, because until very recently this was not thought to be the case. We now know that Chinese beads have a much richer career than had been thought and there are many more Chinese beads available than many people had realized.

Chinese Glass Beads

Most people think of a certain class of beads as being Chinese, and often call them "Peking glass," which is something of a misnomer. The beads are crudely wound from bubbly glass with light perforation deposits. They are often not well shaped and have peaks of glass at the ends, large holes and a distinctive pallet of colors.

The colors are associated with Beijing, and the term "Peking colors" is more appropriate than "Peking glass." The colors were developed under Imperial patronage in Beijing during the late 1600s and the 1700s. One Emperor established workshops in the capital and a later one continued to encourage innovations in glass and glazes. The colors were developed locally and are typical of Chinese glass from this time onward, though they could be made by others and were imitated, especially in Bohemia.

After the fall of the Manchus, the Chinese reacted against their erstwhile foreign overlords. One result was the breaking up of court beads and the selling of the beads individually. They are better made and more precise than their cheaper counterparts made for the common people and export. 19th century.

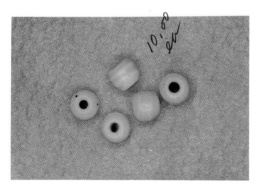

Chinese beads came to the New World centuries ago via Manila, the Philippines, on Spanish Galleons. These simple wound beads are called "Padre beads" in the American southwest, as it is said they were brought to the area by Catholic missionaries from New Spain or Mexico.

Typical Chinese glass exports were rings, made for handles on sewing baskets, pulls for windowshades and other decorative uses. They came in the same palette of colors as the beads. Early 20th century.

The other characteristics of these beads simply reflect the way they were made. Melted glass was poured onto a rod (sometimes even a thin bamboo was used) coated with clay to help the beads come off afterwards. Because the glass was not very hot, it did not always form nicely rounded beads, it remained bubbly and peaks of glass were often left on the ends.

However, in any collection of Chinese glass beads there will be some which are much more perfectly made. They have similar colors, sometimes in more unusual combinations. They are more carefully worked and not as crude as the majority. These beads were for a special purpose. They were used as part of the "court chains" which every official and military officer had to wear during the Manchu or Qing dynasty (1644-1911). These strands, sometimes called "mandarin chains," were modeled after Tibetan rosaries. They could be made from any material as long as it was not specifically reserved for the Emperor. Glass was a great favorite.

Not only did officials and military officers of a certain rank have to wear these beads, but so did their family members, wives wearing three at a time. Different colors were required for different occasions. When the Revolution of 1911 threw off the hated foreign yoke of the Manchus, the Chinese quickly cut off their pigtails (a sign of submission) and broke up the strings of court chains. These beads then entered the market along with the more commercial ones made for export, and are the finest of their type. Most are simple round beads, but special pieces, including pendants and large pancake-shaped counterweights, were also parts of the chains.

These two types of beads with Peking colors are by no means the only kinds of Chinese glass beads made. Their most popular beads for centuries were small simple wound beads which look like tiny sections of a spring and are called "coil beads." These have been exported since the ninth century, and are still living heirloom beads among the Akha in northern Thailand. Another bead popular with the Akha is round with a "crumb" decoration of many tiny bits of glass melted into the surface.

Several types of Chinese beads reached the American market, as we have noted. Some remain heirlooms in isolated villages in Mexico. Perhaps the most widespread type is a simple turquoise blue wound bead. In the American northwest in the early 1800s, explorers Lewis and Clark found them called *tia commoshack*, the "Chief bead" because it was regarded as the chief of all beads. The same bead is found in the American southwest, coming up from Mexico. It is popularly called the "Padre bead" because Spanish missionaries are said to have brought it, whether true or not. Unfortunately, some dealers call any monochrome wound bead a Padre; the name should be reserved only for Chinese beads of this date.

Early in this century and perhaps even before, the Chinese widened their repertoire to include more fancy beads, millefiori (one type of which was used also in paperweights) and aventurine. A variety of Chinese beads and rings, used as handles and pulls are to be found, especially on old imported sewing baskets. And, of course, the Chinese are still making glass beads today.

We do not know where all Chinese beads were made, though in recent centuries most were produced in the Shandong peninsula and inland all the way to Beijing. Quangzhou (Canton) was another area for beadmaking. Archaeological evidence from the 1300s and historical references from the mid-1600s indicate that Boshan in Shandong has long been a major center, though many neighboring towns also made beads. The earliest records of Canton are from the mid 1800s, though we do not know when the industry started. Other places are known to have made beads earlier, but how long they flourished remains to be learned. Unfortunately, independent research within China is currently out of the question.

Other Chinese Beads

In addition to glass, the Chinese have used many media to make beads and other forms of adornment. Jade is considered the finest material for this purpose, and jade beads, toggles, amulets and sew-on pieces were carved in great numbers. When a lower market of less wealthy people was to be reached, glass or jade substitutes such as bowenite, a type of serpentine, were employed.

The Chinese excel at carvings, and beads carved from soft stone or fruit pits are often wonders of dexterity. Enameling was introduced to China from the West centuries ago, and Chinese enamel work is often quite beautiful. Much of the early enameling is dominated by blue, which recalls the beloved Kingfisher feathers, which were glued onto jewelry to impart colors to it. Some enamel work has no cells to separate the colors, while in others wire cells or cloissons were used.

All sorts of materials have been and are still used for Chinese beads. Older jewelry pieces were often elaborately made and decorated with tiny pieces of the brilliant blue Kingfisher feather, obtained from Southeast Asia. Ceramic beads are a very popular line these days, with new designs being developed all the time. Some beads are put together from scraps of sawdust or whatever and simply referred to as "composition" in the West. The variety seems limitless from the world's largest country. Modern China understands the global market for gems and ornaments, and is encouraging geological and artistic activity to bring greater prosperity to the nation.

Chinese glass beads produced in the mid-1980s. They are still made in the old way, retaining some of their charming colors. Note the small coil beads on the strand with the large metal pendant with bells.

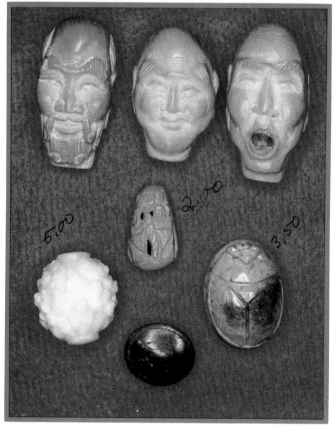

The Chinese have long excelled in carving materials. The heads carved from pits at the top are three Lohan, Buddhist saints, which come in a set of 18. The small pit in the center has several figures. The round white stone bead is called 1000 heads, because so many tiny heads are carved into it. Ironically, the Chinese carve hard stone scarabs for export; the reverse often has pseudo hieroglyphics, as does the small amethyst one at bottom.

Jade is an old favorite with the Chinese. This hat ornament has jade leaves and small wound glass beads. 19th century.

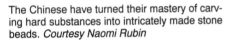

The Chinese have turned their mastery of carving hard substances into intricately made stone beads. *Courtesy Naomi Rubin*

Antique Chinese painted enamels. Translucent colored glass was often applied to small gold, silver or copper jewelry pieces. Blue was favored for resembling precious Kingfisher feathers. The dragon at top was to be sewed onto clothing. The drum pendant under it has the eight trigrams of the *I-Ching*. The central portion of the necklace, perhaps put together recently, includes carnelian pendants and a tiny temple with moving door handles and a small meditating figure inside.

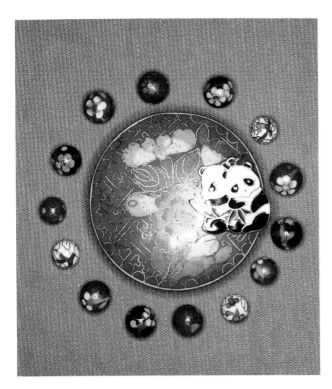

Chinese cloissone enamel is most common today. The large center piece is the top of an old box. The panda pendant was made in Xian and the floral beads in Shanghai, both about 1985.

Complex Chinese pendant, probably of the 19th century. The gilded brass is further decorated with pieces of bright blue kingfisher feathers. The center is a woven pad of tiny coral beads.

The ancient Chinese art of porcelain has been turned to good use with an ever increasing supply of porcelain beads. They include those with traditional blue and white designs and others with more complex polychromes. *Courtesy: Naomi Rubin.*

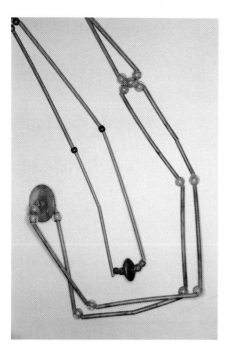

During the puritanical Yi dynasty (1392-1910) Korea was known as the Hermit Kingdom. Beads and other ostentation were discouraged. One use was for the strings that held the men's fragile lacquered silk or horse hair hats on. The long beads are bamboo. The others on the outer string are glass, likely Chinese; those on the inner string are wood.

BEADS IN KOREA

The Korean peninsula may be overshadowed geographically by China, but Koreans are not Chinese, and they have valiantly maintained their independent vision for many centuries. Prehistoric dwellers in Korea used beads widely and even developed a special pendant that became a national symbol. By historic times the Land of the Morning Calm was awash in beads.

The royal tombs of the Three Kingdoms which competed for power on the peninsula for 700 years are full of beads of many different kinds. A few may have been locally made, but most were imported. China provided some. Southeast Asia sent the bulk, especially numerous Indo-Pacific beads, and others came all the way from the Mediterranean world.

During this period Korea made its first glass, though not a very successful product. They used it for only one sort of bead, a pendant shaped like a comma, known in Korea as *gokuk* and in Japan, which adapted it later, as *magatama* (crooked bead). This style, which can be traced to the Korean Neolithic, was principally made with jade. But there was such a demand for it, including many for elaborate gold crowns, that the Koreans learned to make some of glass themselves.

After the wealth of beads during the early dynasties, Korea became much more austere during the Yi period from 1392 until 1910. At this time Korea turned inward, communicating only with China, the source of the neo-Confucianism of the Yi. It came to be called the "Hermit Kingdom," which aptly described the isolationist and puritan attitude of the country. Sumptuary laws were in force, and beads were not encouraged.

Such circumstances did not enhance the markets for beads, but they continued to be used, though in subdued form. Country women, especially shamans, wore them on beaded caps. In the usual dress of the people, beads were employed functionally. They decorated the strings that secured the men's lacquered silk or horse hair top hats. Special beads were used on the ribbon for a boy's pony tail. Beads were sewn onto caps for brides, and women wore beads in their elaborate hair pins. And there were always Buddhist prayer strands. Some beads were local, such as wooden ones or bamboo sections, pearls or "amber" (actually a copal from the *Seoul* or Korean pine tree) while the glass ones were imported from China.

In 1910 Japan invaded Korea and proceeded to make it into a subservient colony. The history of the Korean glass bead industry reflects the economic attitude of the dominant country. At first Japanese beads were sent to Korea for stringing. In 1927, five Korean youths were taken to Japan and taught the art of beadmaking. They returned in the 1930s and opened small factories, some of which still exist. Many of the beads they made (and still make) were sent to Japan, where they were packaged and marked "Made in Japan" to sell to the world. Korea now has a thriving glass bead industry, which includes not only the traditional drip-winding on suspended wire method but modern mechanized tube drawing machines as well.

Many other beads are currently being made in Korea, too. One of the most charming are made by wrapping silk around a base. This is traditional women's work and still done by them, though the muted colors and wooden cores of the past have been replaced by brighter hues and plastic cores.

Another unusual bead is the product of Japanese technology introduced in the 1960s. These are made of a secret mixture of flour and held together by a special binder. Koreans attend the "Flour Flower Institute" to learn to make these beads. They are laborious to produce and thus expensive, but young Korean women love them.

Modern Korean glass bead production is imaginative and highly varied. The green pendant at top is a Gokuk (Magatama in Japanese), an ancient Korean device. The pig symbolizes wealth. Many of the beads are made from a handsome mottled glass. Note the malachite imitation, the foil bead and the luster coated rectangular blue jewelry element in the center.

Modern glass beads made in Seoul, Korea. The beadmakers were taught the art as youths by being taken to Japan during the occupation of Korea. Many of these beads are made to resemble jade.

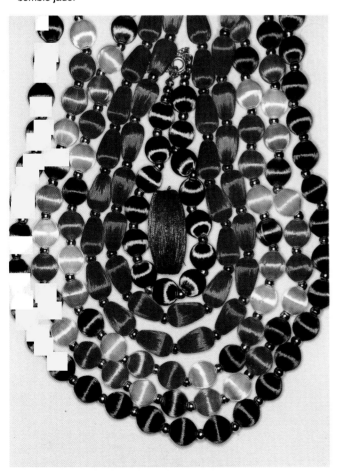

An old Korean craft practiced by women was winding silk threads around a wooden bead. Today the base is plastic. The bead in the center is an old one; the others modern.

Beginning in the 1960s the Koreans learned to make another bead from the Japanese, with a secret mixture of flour (farina) and glues. Koreans study the technique at the Flour Flower Institute in Korea. Expensive and fragile, they are great favorites with young Korean women.

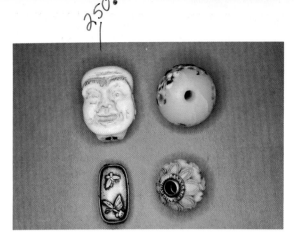

250°

Japanese ojime are beads used to secure the top of a pocket-like inro, a small box worn with a kimino. The elaborately carved or decorated ojime here are made of ivory, silver and glass. *Courtesy of Rita Okrent.*

5.00
10.00

3.— 4.00 ea

Japanese foil beads. As European beadmakers produced fewer and fewer foil beads, the Japanese stepped into the market on an increasing scale. The pink bead in the center is a great favorite, but no longer made.

2.00

Delicately made glass birds and fish are products of the Japanese lamp-winding bead industry. Late 1970s.

Beads are also made from many other materials, including stones. Caution should be exercised, as Korea jade is really bowenite serpentine, smoky topaz is really smoky quartz, and at least some of their amethysts are synthetic. Korea's economic boom includes a thriving jewelry industry, and we may see many more interesting beads from Korea in the near future.

BEADS IN JAPAN

Being an archipelago, Japan was able to maintain its independence from giant China, but it continuously received influences, from not only China but also Korea. Beads, including glass beads, are found for a long time in Japan. The early ones were probably imports, though local production is possible, especially considering the Japanese tendency to improve upon any imports they admire.

In the eighth century Nara period there was apparently a flourishing Japanese bead industry. Many of the 75,000 beads enshrined with Emperor Shomu in the Shoso-in temple in 765 are thought to be of Japanese origin. The Shoso-in temple is a unique monument to its time. It is still reverently preserved with all the treasures of the honored monarch, and is not available for general viewing, but only opened and aired out once every few years.

Beadmaking declined after the Nara period, not to resume again until the Edo period (1615-1867). Edo Japan used beads as decorations on many articles, including hair combs and beaded curtains, but the most celebrated of them were accessories to the *inro*. The inro was a small box with various compartments which took the place of pockets, being attached to the pocketless kimono. To keep the inro secured to the sash of the kimono a toggle or netsuke was employed, and to keep the top of the inro firmly closed against the base a sliding bead or ojime was used.

Netsuke and Ojime are collected by bead lovers, though some favor one over the other. The Netsuke was most often carved of ivory with a special V-shaped perforation in back. Ojime were commonly made of glass by Edo artisans. Many other materials have been used for both. During the Edo period, the Ojime and other beads became more and more elaborate.

Japanese beads have received different names, based upon their appearance. *Tombodama* means "dragonfly bead" because of its elaborate decoration, while *Sarasadama* were also elaborate but more delicate; they are named for imported Indian textiles. *Magatama*, which we discussed above, is another common bead-pendant. All these names have *dama* (gem) as their root.

The modern Japanese bead industry began after Japan was "opened" to the rest of the world by Commodore Perry of the United States in 1853. In the 1870s Sakubei Oi began beadmaking after he had studied in Europe and run a factory in India. He produced different glass beads and introduced artificial pearls to Japan. By the 1880s pearl making had been improved and the qualities were better. Japan makes fine artificial pearls today.

Another chapter in the Japanese bead story is their perfection of cultured pearls. By inserting something into an oyster shell, one can induce the animal to cover it with nacre, a trick the Chinese had known for centuries. However, it was not until Kokichi Mikimoto developed perfectly round cultured pearls in the late 1800s that the world recognized a new gem. Japanese cultured pearls now dominate the market. Japan also furnishes cultured freshwater pearls, the attractively misshapen Biwa pearls, named for the lake of their origin.

Much glass beadmaking was done by farmers at home during leisure time. Glass was supplied to them, and this was melted by a lamp and trailed onto a suspended wire which was twirled either with one hand or a treadle. Such wound beads remain a staple of Japanese production. Molding was also introduced, as were drawing techniques.

At least some Japanese bead production was done abroad. We mentioned above how the Japanese repackage Korean beads in their own name. Long drawn tubes which have not been reheated on the ends, commonly blue and sometimes silvered inside, are probably joint products of Japan and China. Both places seem to have made them, but even before the Japanese invasion of Manchuria and occupation of China in the 1930s, several Chinese glass beadmaking factories were owned or run by Japanese.

The present Japanese bead industry is one of the strongest in the world. They continue to make wound and molded beads. They have aggressively moved into making small drawn seed beads, and are generally considered the best as well as the biggest producers today. Production is largely geared to export, and Japan seems to be determined to become the great bead power of the next century.

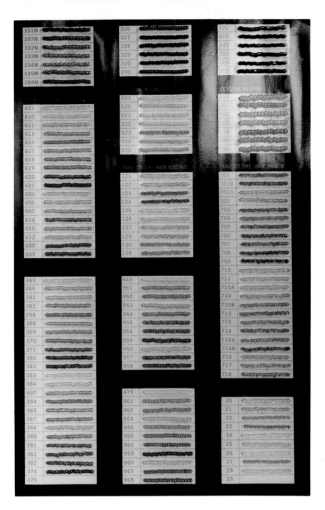

Handwound Japanese beads. The strand of small red beads was made in occupied Japan after World War II. The others are more recent. Note the complex lattice-work bead in white and blue.

The Japanese have moved quickly to secure for themselves a dominant position in much of the world's market for small drawn "seed beads." This sample card shows just some of the variety they offer.

The Japanese have become major players in the world glass bead market. The string of drawn and blown beads was made shortly after World War II. The molded beads in the center are more recent. The "seed beads" outside the string are delicia beads, popularly called "delicious" in the U.S.; their uniformity and large holes make them favorites with beadworkers.

Beads made by the late Japanese master Kyuyo Asao in the 1970s and early 1980s. The precision of his work has made his beads very collectible. *Courtesy Albert Summerfield.*

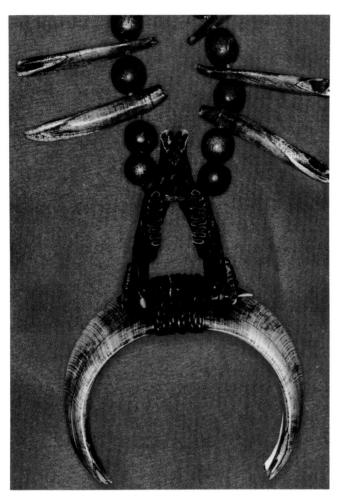

A necklace of a medicine man among the Bontoc of northern Luzon, the Philippines. The round beads are wood and the long pendants between them animal teeth. The crescent at the end is made of two boar tusks tied to the lower jaw of the local cloud rat.

This exotic corner of the world is quickly becoming a focus for bead collecting. This is so for several reasons. There are many groups in Southeast Asia who have valued beads for centuries and kept them as heirlooms. Some of these heirlooms are very old, and unlike beads illegally looted from archaeological sites, there is no ethical objection to collecting them.

Southeast Asia is also booming economically and many people there are beginning to collect beads and to organize bead societies. Academics in museums and universities are also awakening to the value of beads in their studies. Finally, there are a number of different beadmaking industries.

The story of beads in Southeast Asia is particularly exciting, because the islands and peninsulas of the region have been the recipients of beads from much of the world for thousands of years. We shall begin with a brief historical look at beads in the area and then discuss its collectible beads.

BEAD HISTORY IN SOUTHEAST ASIA

Southeast Asia is geographically caught between the great powers of India and China, reflected even in some names: Indochina, Indonesia (the Indian islands). India was the first historical influence there; traders introduced their goods along with their ideas of philosophy, religion and statehood. Even in the first century, ancient ports as far away as Bali received glass drawn Indo-Pacific beads and stone and glass beads that are recognizably Indian.

The first state in Southeast Asia was Funan, centered in southern Vietnam. Its great port, Oc-eo, and its western port Takkola (now called Klong Thom in southern Thailand, though locally known as Khuan Lukpad or "bead hill") were important beadmakers, both of Indo-Pacific beads and stone beads. Other states developed in the early centuries A.D. as well, some of them like Ho-ling in Java mostly importing beads and others such as the Pyu kingdom in Myanmar (Burma) producing many of their own. About the seventh century, Funan fell to the Khymers, and leadership shifted south.

Srivijaya, based in Palembang, Sumatra, extended its hold over Sumatra, much of Java and the Malay peninsula. The capital city itself was a beadmaker of note, producing Indo-Pacific beads, stone beads and glass beads either made by or taught by early Arab traders. Beads from the Islamic West were imported. Several other cities of Srivijaya also made glass and stone beads. Srivijaya, like Funan before it, was the trading link between the West and India on one hand and China on the other. One of its key ports was Sungai Mas ("Golden River") in Malaysia, where locally made and imported beads have been found in great numbers.

The fall of Srivijayan power around 1200 left a void in the Southeast Asian bead trade. Indo-Pacific beads were no longer as commonly available as before. Soon thereafter trade from the Arab world slowed to a trickle, and their exotic beads were no longer being imported.

But just at that time China began to trade actively with the region, sailing in Chinese ships with Chinese crews. Soon Chinese traders were everywhere, and they took beads with them. There are books written for Chinese sailors in the 1200s and 1300s instructing them where to go and what to use in trade. Glass beads figured prominently as trade items throughout Southeast Asia.

By the 1500s the Europeans were making their presence felt. They came as traders and stayed on as colonists. They brought their own beads, though in some regions Chinese traders and beads continued to dominate for centuries. European beads grew in popularity, but many of the older beads remained, especially among people in more isolated, mountainous regions. Following World War II and Independence, many countries of the region developed strong bead industries of their own.

HEIRLOOM BEADS IN SOUTHEAST ASIA

When we think of heirlooms we envision something old and nice that we get from grandmother. It is not the same heirloom our neighbor has, because each family has its own. In Southeast Asia, particularly among isolated minorities occupying marginal mountainous lands, heirlooms are quite different. Their fate is closely regulated by the community, because they are not privately owned, but kept in trust for all. Everyone in a village knows which heirlooms everyone else has. Strict rules govern their care, use and inheritance. Beads, along with old ceramics and bronzes, are the most common heirlooms.

In some cases, these heirlooms are as much as a thousand years old, having been handed down for many generations. These old beads include a few from the Mediterranean world highly valued among the Kayan of Borneo, whose most valued bead is estimated to be worth $4,000 — per bead, if you can get someone to sell it to you.

The commoners of the eastern islands in Indonesia, including Flores, Sumba, Timor and others, value reddish brown Indo-Pacific beads, which are inherited through the sons and used as bride-price. They were likely made in Srivijaya and are 800 or so years old, yet they are fairly cheap. The princely families of the same islands have another reddish-brown bead which they used as bride-wealth: the small Chinese coil bead. It is considered so valuable that commoners aren't even allowed to touch them. Both types fall under the general name of Mutisalah (false pearl), though each has specific names and duties.

An assortment of beads on the Indonesian market. The strands of white hearts and yellow beads are worn in Irian Jaya (on New Guinea) by brides. On top is a bead of dendritic limestone from Borneo, often erroneously called fossil bone or ivory. The two yellow beads below it were made by the powder-glass method in Borneo in the 1930s; note the perforations. The lamp-wound beads to their right were Venetian attempts to imitate the Lukut Sekala, a bead worth over $4000. Below the yellow beads are two Chinese wound beads. Below them is a blue bead made by Chinese living in Java around 1600, now an heirloom in Borneo. To its right is a 15th century bead acknowledged to be old, but not appreciated, called the "ghost bead." The striped beads on bottom are Venetian from the 1870s made to imitate an earlier bead with a similar pattern of stripes.

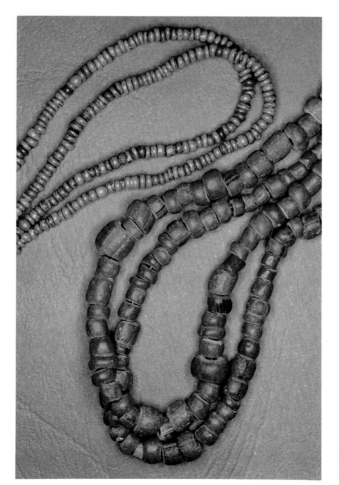

In eastern Indonesian islands such as Timor, Flores and Sumba, reddish brown glass beads serve as valued heirlooms collectively called Mutisalah (false pearls). Those of the common people are drawn Indo-Pacific beads, called Mutitanah (earth pearls) when red or Mutibata (brick pearls) when orange, 800 or more years old. Those of the princely families are small wound Chinese coil beads called Mutiraja (King's pearls), probably some 500 years old.

1.25 ea

The valued beads among the Chin of Myanmar (Burma) and their cousins the Kuki and related groups on the Indian (western) side are called Pumtek (buried thunderbolt). Genuine ones around 1000 to 1500 years old were made from opalized (fossilized) palm wood, evident by dark striations along the sides, as on the two beads to the left. Imitations have been made since about 1926 from fossilized (but not opalized) hard wood, with finer grains.

Among the Chin of western Burma and their cousins, the Kukis of eastern India, the honored bead is the Pumtek ("buried thunderbolt"). The old ones were made by the Pyu, perhaps 1000 years ago, by adding dark patterns onto beads cut from opalized (petrified) palm wood. At the beginning of this century, villagers living near an ancient Pyu city began looting its graveyard and sold off the old beads to the Chin, who flocked to the village annually to buy them. When they ran out they began making copies on petrified (but not opalized) hard-grained wood. Both are now on the market, the genuine ones being much more valuable.

In northern Luzon, the largest island in the Philippines, several neighboring groups honor heirloom beads, but they do not cherish the same ones. The Kalinga and Gad-dang have mostly European beads of the last century as heirlooms, while the Ifugao keep primarily older Chinese beads, some of them 500 years in age. Heirloom beads of the Bontoc are carnelians (which all these people like) and locally cut large white marble beads. These are worn on the heads of Bontoc women, who also wear a strand of python vertebrae to keep lightening away.

Old Chinese beads are important to several groups, including the Paiwan of Taiwan, the Akha of northern Thailand and the Kelebit of Borneo. In many cases, we can trace something of the history of people with heirloom beads. The ages of these beads often, but not always, are very close to the period when they faced a crises in their existence and were forced to strengthen their own ethnic identity in order to survive as a community.

There are also different ways of keeping heirloom beads. Some people hand them down to one descendent, while others divide their collections between several heirs. Some have closed collections, to which new beads can never be added. Others maintain open collections, adding new beads over time each generation or so. A necklace from the Toraja of Sulawesi (the Celebes) in Indonesia demonstrates both an open collection and the dividing of beads among heirs over many generations; it may have beads ranging in date from 500 years to 100 or even newer.

Chinese beads are favored heirlooms among the Akha of northern Thailand, whose homeland is in Yunnan, China. The inner beads are coil beads, made by twisting a little glass around a wire over a heat too low to consolidate the bead or to remove the peaks of glass at the ends.

Strand of heirloom beads of the southern Toraja people of Sulawesi (the Celebes), Indonesia. The strand has a great variety of beads, ranging from 15th century Chinese, 17th century Dutch and 19th century Czech, with Chinese and Venetian beads of various ages. The beads have been carefully handed down through generations.

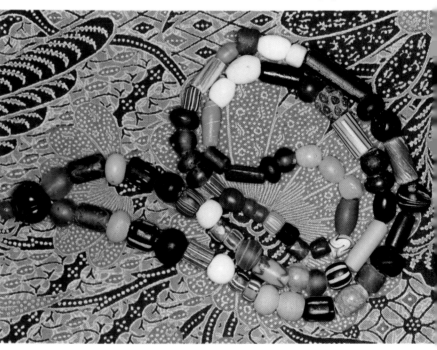

AMULETS IN THAILAND

As we discussed in Chapter Three, the use of beads for amulets is one of their most important functions. While the great center of amulets in the ancient world was Egypt, the society which uses most today is Thailand. Amulets are worn by Thais of all classes. Not all are beads, some of them take other forms, including tattooing. They come in a great variety, and we can only discuss some of the more common and interesting ones.

The most widespread Thai amulet consists of small votive tablets, most commonly of clay, which have been molded with a figure of Buddha on it. These were originally made by monks and deposited in Buddhist stupas, but in time came to be regarded as talismans. When ancient tablets are found they are considered very potent, and one can see knots of men on the sidewalk closely examining such tablets with magnifying glasses and discussing whether they are genuine or not. Newer tablets are made by the thousands and range from very cheap to expensive, depending on their workmanship and who made them. One or more are commonly worn around the neck in small boxes of plastic or metal, including gold for the best ones.

No longer as popular as they once were, many men still wear the *palad khik*, a phallus-shaped amulet, around the waist. Some have large collections and wear many at once. These are usually made of wood, but other materials are also used, and they are sometimes inscribed with old Khymer letters (Thai characters are never used on amulets). Their origin is probably from the worship of the linga in Hinduism, but now they are considered protectors against evil and bringers of strength.

The *luk om* is an amulet which is round and can fit in the mouth. Most commonly it is a large, heavy bead interesting because of its material. Though they can be made of many things, the most favored one is solidified mercury, made by a complex formula.

Many other items are considered magical and potent in Thailand, including almost any unusual natural object like a fossil or tektite. At the same time, many amulets are made to represent more familiar objects to fulfill specific functions. Prayers (always written in Khymer script) are effective by themselves, and metal strips upon which prayers have been scratched or embossed may be rolled up and worn as beads.

The Thais pay great attention to amulets. Most common are small Buddhist clay votive figures. The phallic *palad khik* is worn by men. At bottom is a *luk om* made of solidified mercury. The monkey is an amulet for scholars. The painted and gilded beads are made of clay.

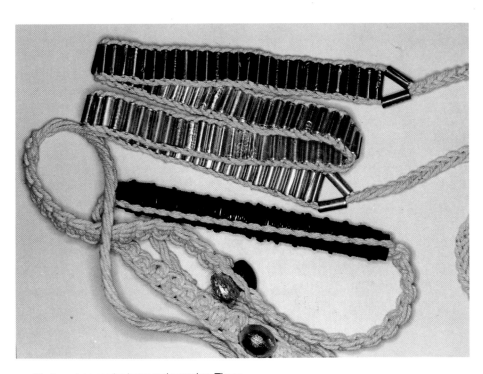

Thai amulets can be large and complex. These two belts contain metal plates (one wound into a single large bead, the other a series of small tubular beads) impressed with prayers in Khymer script.

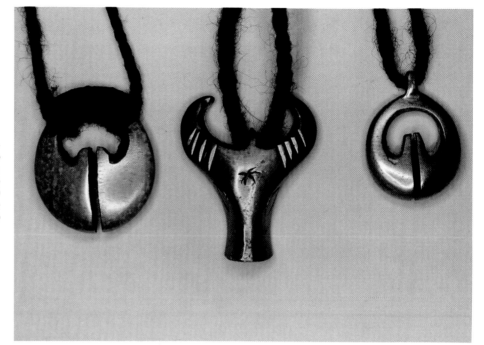

Cast bronze and silver (gold is also used) pendants made by the Ifugao of northern Luzon, the Philippines. The water buffalo head is a modern adaptation. However, the split circle or **C** shape style (called Bung) dates back 2000 to 3000 years. Originally an earring, neighbors of the Ifugao still wear them in their ears, but the Ifugao use them principally as pendants.

Metalworking is found throughout South and Southeast Asia. The two beads at top were made by Khymers of Cambodia, but now mostly in Thailand. The center is lac and metal is placed over that and decorated. The filigree pipal leaf and flower are from Cuttack, Orissa, India and similar to work done in Malaysia. The square brass bead is favored by the Akha of Thailand. The silver bead below decorated with granulation was made at Celuk, Bali, Indonesia.

MODERN BEADS IN SOUTHEAST ASIA

All through Southeast Asia are many places where beads of different types are made. Some of the beadmakers are inheritors of very ancient practices, while others have newly developed their skills. They fulfill the demands of their local markets, and the more successful ones are geared toward export.

Metal Beads

Probably the oldest metalworking bead industry is rather isolated in the mountains of northern Luzon in the Philippines. Among the Ifugao are smiths who use bronze, silver and gold to cast ornaments locally called *bung* or *lingling-o*. These are worn by some local people as earrings and by others as pendants. The **C**-form of these pendants recalls earrings brought to the islands 2000 to 3000 years ago by ancient mariners. The ancient ones were made of jade, but the Philippines is rich in gold and copper, and these materials were adapted to make these unique adornments.

Another ancient craft is practiced in the village of Ban Kwow (Ban means village) in northern Thailand. Khymer craftsmen, mostly recent refugees from Pat Pol's Cambodia, continue an art they have practiced for a thousand years or so. Thin ribbons of silver and gold (now mostly gold wash on silver) are formed into beads and then filled with lac. The lac keeps the beads firm. When the bead has been completed, sharpened nails and such tools are used to engrave designs on the sides. The results are complex and attractive beads made in a unique ancient style.

There is gold working in most parts of Southeast Asia, but silver working is usually more closely connected to beads and pendants. In Nakorn Si Thammarat, Thailand, there is a lively niello industry. Niello consists of black designs put into silver with compounds made of metals and sulfur. It is an old Western art, but it has been practiced in Thailand and Malaysia for centuries.

Silver working, especially filigree work, is well known from Malaysia, where it is centered in the northeast. It consists of soldering thin wires of silver to each other to build up a light, airy pattern. Malaysia is also home to pewter manufactures, since it is a major producer of tin.

Even more impressive are the shops located in Celuk, Bali, Indonesia, where filigree and granulation are practiced. In granulation tiny balls of metal are soldered to a base to form a pattern. The balls are made by heating very short pieces of hand-drawn wire, gluing them onto the base with the glue from the "coral seed" and carefully soldering them to the base.

Stone Beads

For a very long time India supplied beads of semiprecious stones to Southeast Asia. However, stone beadmaking has been carried on in a number of places in the region for many centuries. Some of the beadmakers seem to have supplied only local markets, while others may have traded their beads further. The beads made at ancient Srivijaya, for example, are found throughout the Srivijayan kingdom.

Bangkok has become a major cutter of precious stones, especially ruby, sapphire and other colored gems. Thailand is rich in these stones, as are several of its neighbors such as Burma and Cambodia. The Asian Institute of Geological Studies has been founded there as the only branch of the Gemological Institute of America. With the combination of gems, favorable customs laws and the expertise gained at AIGS, Bangkok has become the "Colored Gem Stone Capital of the World." Little of this activity consists of bead cutting, but some of the larger commercial houses are beginning to make beads.

At several places in Indonesia beadmaking has come to be an important industry. Sukabumi in Java has long been a source of semiprecious stones, especially agates. Owners of a number of small factories there cut beads, many of them having learned from the large, modern factory near Bogor, called Tiasky Emms.

In addition to Sukabumi-Bogor, there are smaller lapidaries elsewhere in Indonesia. Those making beads are located at Pacitan, in East Java and Pengkabaru, Sumatra. At Padang, Sumatra and Carita, West Java are stone workers, making mostly gems for rings. Some stone beads from local materials, such as dendritic limestone (often erroneously identified as "fossils") is going on in Borneo. While the beads in mechanized factories such as Tiasky Emms are well cut, those of some of the smaller centers are not as skillfully made.

Glass Beadmaking

Indonesia, the giant of the region, is the only country making many glass beads. The collector must be warned, however, that there is a considerable industry there dedicated to imitating ancient beads for sale on the antiquities market. Some of these are more-or-less skillfully done. Others are fairly obvious because they are not made of glass at all, but plaster or other compositions.

A minor bead industry in Indonesia is concerned with imitations of ancient beads. Top right is a glass bead imitating an ancient mosaic bead (center). Top left is a bead made of plaster. Bottom left is an ancient drawn bead incised with the design of the ancient "bird bead;" the lines were filled with some soluble paste. At bottom right is a genuine ancient small bicone in green glass and an imitation in black colored plaster.

Stones from the nearby river are brought to the village of Pacitan, Java, Indonesia where they are chipped, ground and polished against bamboo to form into beads. The finish is usually not very precise, but the beads have a rustic sort of charm not seen in the production of some more sophisticated stone bead centers.

The largest new glass beadmaking industry in the world is at Plumbon Gambang in eastern Java. Little more than a decade old, it now employs some 250 villagers, who melt waste glass, draw it into canes and form lamp-wound beads, often with sophisticated designs.

In the village of Plumbon Gambang, East Java, there is a flourishing glass bead industry, probably the largest such new industry in the world. When Solekan (many Javanese have only one name) retired from a light bulb factory in nearby Surabaya in the 1970s he tried his hand at working small glass objects. In a few years he and his son, Sudarto, were making glass "stones" for rings and then beads. The industry grew. Scrap glass is bought from factories in Surabaya, stretched by hand into long canes, and then melted at lamps by workers. Asbestos is/was used as the separator (I warned Sudarto against this). The beads are nicely made and prettily decorated, especially with a variety of combed designs.

When I asked Sudarto who bought the beads he replied that Japan and Saudi Arabia were his biggest customers. The museum people who had taken me to the village were surprised about Saudi Arabia, but I explained that Mecca has been a major bead mart for many centuries. "Yes," Sudarto related, "a man from the next village came back from making his pilgrimage and was anxious to show me a strand of prayer beads he had bought in Mecca. I told him we make them in our village." Beads do get around.

Plastic Beads

Plastics are treated as a raw material for beadmaking by several people in Southeast Asia. These are not urban dwellers, but minority groups living in relatively isolated regions. One motive for making these beads is to preserve their own heirloom beads. By selling the plastic imitations they are not forced to sell their old beads.

Two of these groups are located in the Philippines. The Kalinga of northern Luzon have been making plastic beads at least since the 1960s. Current production is rather sophisticated, resembling their heirloom strands. These are taken by the villagers of Lubuagan, who make them, to other Kalinga villages, where they are worn mostly by children and the poor. They are also occasionally seen for sale outside the region.

In the south of the country the T'boli, who live near Lake Sebu on Mindanao Island, also make plastic beads. They began producing in the 1960s as well, and had gone through several stages of styles by the early 1990s. Strands made in the 1980s resembled their important heirloom beads, and were further decorated with brass chains and bells, which they also make by the lost wax method. Both the Kalinga and T'boli buy plastic combs, rulers and other items at local markets, heat them and shape them into beads.

In central Borneo in Indonesia another sort of bead is made with a core of a composition that looks mostly like sawdust which has been covered with a layer of plastic. I don't have any more details on these yet. Though I regard them as some of the least attractive beads in the Center's collection, some visitors love them. I acquired them in Jakarta after several hours of being hounded by a young dealer, who eventually accepted a mere fraction of his original offering price.

Plastic can be recycled. Two peoples of the Philippines buy combs and rulers in the marketplace, melt them down and make beads that resemble their heirloom glass beads. The four strand necklace is made by the Kalinga of northern Luzon; the two beads below it are from the 1970s. The single strand necklace with lost-wax brass pieces was made by the T'boli of Mindanao in the 1980s. In the 1990s the style changed to the single beads in the center.

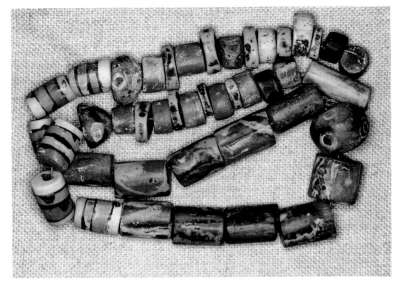

Touted as ancient beads by dealers, these are made of a composition covered with plastic in Central Kalimantan (Borneo), Indonesia. I consider them some of the ugliest beads in the Center's collection; some visitors love them.

Other Materials

One of the principal shell bead industries in the world is on Mactan Island near Cebu City in the central Philippines. (Mactan is where the explorer Magellan was killed in 1521). The industry not only turns the abundant (though some are endangered) shells of the archipelago into beads, but uses many other materials in a bewildering variety, including palm nuts, coconut shell and even carabao (water buffalo) hooves. Inexpensive labor combined with Filipino artistry and abundant raw materials have made this a major exporting business.

Clay beads are made in many places, but perhaps the most notable industry in Southeast Asia is in the village of Ban Dan Kwian, Thailand. Its river is a source of a fine brown clay, which the Mons of the village have been using for pottery for ages. In the late 1960s Sudarat (Thais also commonly use only one name), a recent art school graduate, began trying her hand at beadmaking. A couple of Thai popular rock groups began wearing her creations and soon there was a great demand for them.

On the island of Mactan near Cebu in the Philippines is an active bead industry using a wide variety of local materials. The necklace is made of the outer whorl of many shells. Inside from top to bottom are a bead made by piecing together tiny mother-of-pearl chips, an apple coral, a large coconut disc, a palm seed with natural veins and one each dyed purple and gold, a red dyed coral and a (bleached?) golden coral.

In the village of Tampaksiring, Bali, the old craft of carving sandalwood beads and wall hangings from coconut shell has given birth to a lively industry making colorful jewelry by painting pine wood figures.

A lively clay beadmaking center is established at Ban Dan Kwain, an ancient Mon pottery village in Thailand. The round brown beads are made of the untreated natural clay. The butterfly is incised, washed with a lime coat and colored. The earring is an example of a newer direction the work is heading.

You can't patent clay beadmaking, so in a short time other villagers began making beads, too, and prices dropped. In addition to the local brown clay, a white kaolin is imported from the north, often mixed with commercial colors. Black is achieved by coating beads with coconut oil before firing. The beads are shaped and decorated by almost any means you might imagine; everything is used from acrylic molds for shapes to plastic brushes for texture. Many are colored and really quite attractive. They are not of the highest quality, but Sudarat and others are constantly working on improvements. The beads are popular with young Thai girls, and it won't be long before they are easily bought around the world.

There are, of course, many other beads made in Southeast Asia. When the four countries (Viet Nam, Laos, Cambodia and Burma) which are now generally closed to the outside world open, even more will be available.

CHAPTER ELEVEN
AFRICA

When bead collectors think of Africa, two images come to mind. One is that it produces beads, some of which are sold all over the world. The other is that Africa has long been a major market for beads. The common term, "African Trade Bead," refers to this latter situation. Enormous numbers of mostly European glass beads were traded into the continent during the last few centuries and many of them have come onto the world market since the 1960s.

BACKGROUND

Africa is the cradle of the human race, and beads have been made, traded and used there for many thousands of years. These early beads were made of natural materials, and some of them — doum palm nuts, ostrich eggshells and marine shells among them — are still being used.

The huge continent was relatively unknown to the rest of the outside world until trade began in earnest in the Indian Ocean. Egyptian, Greek and Indian adventurers established trading bases along the East Africa coast as much as 2000 years ago. After the fall of the Roman Empire, Arabs, Persians and Indians continued the commerce.

In West Africa the growing expanse of the Sahara desert kept outsiders away until North African Arabs began to blaze trails south around the eighth century. There they traded with the wealthy kingdom of Ghana mostly located in what is now Mauritania. By the thirteenth century or so, Ghana had been absorbed by the kingdom of Mali, based along the interior Niger delta. The Arabs took mostly salt, copper and bronze and glass beads — especially blue ones — to the African kingdoms; in exchange they received gold and slaves.

These long established patterns were interrupted by the growing naval power of Europe. Beginning in the late 1400s the Portuguese made their way further and further down the West African coast, and by 1498 had rounded the Cape of Good Hope and sailed on to India. For centuries, Europeans were mostly confined to the coasts. The interior was uninviting and suspicious, and rather few intrepid souls attempted to penetrate it.

A strand of beads from West Africa commonly called Dogon (a people living in Mali) or Dutch. The small annular or ring beads are German. The larger beads are probably Venetian, though some may be Dutch or German.

One of the more artistic crafts of Africa is beadmaking from powdered glass. Their value and skill is only beginning to be recognized in the West. These bracelets are made of Krobo beads, each of which was originally made in two halves.

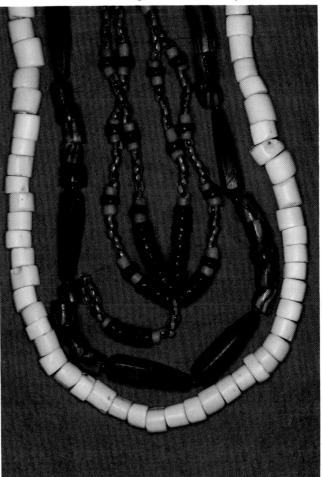

Europeans and Americans greatly accelerated the slave trade, which became a global scandal by the 1800s, when it gradually began to be reduced. At the same time, Europe scrambled for control of Africa, dividing it into unrealistic spheres of influence, most of which were mere inland extensions of the coastal areas they controlled by force. During the colonial period European beads poured into Africa, sometimes reaching as much as 40% of total imports or 2.5 pounds of glass beads for every man, woman and child each year.

Independence came late to most African countries, many of whom still struggle with the residual effects of slavery, impoverishment, balkanization and colonialism. Beads remain very much a part of the African experience in much of the continent. Many people cherish old beads as heirlooms or as markers of every stage of life. Beads are a crucial item of internal commerce, and especially since the 1970s, have become an increasingly lucrative commodity on the international market.

AFRICAN BEAD MARKETS AND ALTERING BEADS

Bead traders in Africa are rarely people who have simply chosen to go into this particular business to work at it for an uncertain length of time. Most bead traders learned their profession at the elbows of their father or mother, and can trace bead selling back in the family for many generations. Thus, they have a proprietary sense of what they are doing.

Within Africa there are people, such as the Hausa in West Africa, who dominate the commerce in beads. Some of them travel long distances to visit remote villages and secure beads, taking them to large market towns or cities to sell to fellow Africans or foreigners. Another duty of many bead traders is that they are responsible for changing or altering some of the beads they handle.

Some beads typical of the African trade. The white beads on the outside are commonly called "porcelain," though they are actually drawn glass. The middle strand is a mixture of Czech imitation carnelians and powder-glass beads. The inner strand has powder-glass beads and small Venetian drawn beads. The two inner strands were probably strung for exporting.

Altering beads by grinding is very common in West Africa. At top are two Venetian yellow glass discs, the right one ground flat to sit nicely on a strand. The next row has a wound yellow heart ground into a hexagonal bicone and a blue bead with mosaic chips beveled on the ends to made a nice strand. The two beads on the bottom have also been beveled and the yellow bead has had most of its decoration removed.

Why is this done? Aesthetics and fashion are certainly reasons. When we also realize that many Africans put a premium on the creativity of Africans themselves, we have another key to the importance of altering beads. By altering we mean changing the bead in some fundamental way after it has left the hands of the manufacturer. This is not limited to Africa, but we know far more examples of it there than in America or Asia. Nor is it a new phenomenon; by 1605 it was flourishing in West Africa. Hence, understanding this process is vital for understanding beads exported from Africa.

There are two major ways of altering beads. One is by grinding them against stones. This is usually done to make the beads on a strand fit together well, either by grinding them lengthwise to make them all smooth and the same diameter or by grinding them flat and beveled on the ends so they sit snugly on a strand. Grinding is also used to remove glass decorations (not everyone likes patterns on their beads) or to reshape the bead.

The most interesting story of grinding beads began with the importing of old style wound Hebron opaque yellow and green beads to Egypt. From there they went up the Nile to kingdoms in what are now Sudan and Chad beginning in the 1700s. These beads, locally called *mongur*, were greatly admired by the women. By the late 1800s Hebron changed its glassmaking (see Chapter Eight). By the 1930s the beads, which had not been available for 50 years, had gone out of fashion and itinerant Hausa bead traders bought them for a song. They took them home to Kano, Nigeria, and ground the rounded ends flat. Today they sell them in Khartoum at steep prices to the granddaughters of the women who once gave them away, calling them "Kano beads." It was once thought that they were made in Kano, but we know now they were only altered there.

The other major bead altering process is done with heat. This is carried out by mixing beads with organic matter in a pot and heating them over a charcoal fire for about an hour. Beads treated this way change their appearance. Translucent ones become cloudy, are deformed a bit, and often have grooves along the side where stretched air bubbles of the drawn beads break open. The best known bead to which this is done is the tubular blue Koli bead from Ghana, especially because of its relationship with the famous Aggrey bead. However, the Koli is by no means the only bead so treated.

BEADMAKING

Powder-glass Beadmaking

This method of making beads involves crushing glass very fine and heating it so that the particles fuse together. This technique is known from several societies, including East and West Africa some 1000 years ago, the Mandan and Arikara of North America and in Borneo. The most important representatives in our day are in West Africa, especially in Ghana. Collectors sometimes call these "pot beads," "sand cast beads" or "priest's beads." None of these names are appropriate since they are not cast or made in pots and have nothing to do with sand or priests.

The process begins with glass, usually scrap bottles which are pounded into a fine powder. The glass is then poured into clay molds, which have cells poked into them for the beads. At the bottom of each cell is a small depression into which the leaf stem of a cassava plant is placed. The powder is poured into the molds in various ways depending on the design wanted. Once a couple dozen molds are filled they go into crude ovens and a fire is lit in it for about an hour. The glass coalesces and the cassava stems burn out, leaving a perforation. When finished, the beads are shaken from the molds, cleaned and sometimes polished.

In Ghana this work is done in several villages in Asante territory in the central region and other villages in the Krobo lands of the southeast. Though there is some overlap, there is enough variety to distinguish production of one village from another. Ghanaians have been making these beads at least since the 1600s and possibly long before. Some of the older beads, such as those made in long horizontal molds, are now highly regarded, because no one is making them any more.

As Hebron beads went out of fashion in the Sudan by the 1930s Hausa traders bought them up for a song. They took them home and ground the ends to flatten and bevel them. They now sell them in Sudan at steep prices to the granddaughters of the women who once gave them away, calling them Kano beads after the Hausa capital.

Altering is also commonly done with heat. At top right is a short blue Czech tube of the type heated into Koli beads in Ghana. Below it are two examples of Koli beads; note the breaking out of air bubbles along the side. The two small beads at top are ancient Indo-Pacific beads flattened by heating; below them is a Venetian bead treated in the same way. The large striped bead at the bottom was heated in the same way as the Koli beads.

A typical array of Ghanaian powder-glass beads on a mold. The outer strand is Asante; the inner one Krobo. The groups on the mold clockwise from left: the Asante village of Ohwim; the Asante village of Asamang; the Krobo village of Aboabo; the Asante village of Dabaa; the Asante village of Abrade.

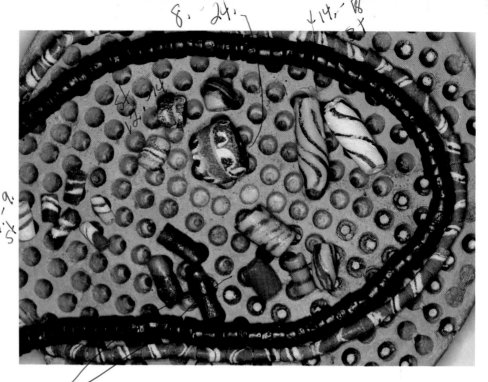

Some older Ghanaian powder-glass beads. The five at the top were made in a horizontal mold (note the pattern of lines and the shape of the bead in cross section). Yellow is most common; the other colors are scarcer. The bead with the banded layers (one is shown end on) is called Awarypa and favored by the Asante at weddings. The two larger beads with longitudinal stripes are of the type commonly worn around the waist.

Another powder-glass bead industry is worked by women in Mauritania, centered around the town of Kiffa. Instead of heating crushed glass in a mold, some glass is mixed with a binder (sugar, gum arabic, even saliva) and a core is formed. Onto this core delicate designs are carefully added in powdered glass and the whole fired. Sometimes plain European beads are used directly as the core. The striking designs on these small beads have made them very desirable and expensive.

Some of the most valuable beads in West Africa are very old powder-glass beads. These include the Bodom, made on a dark core, probably formed with an organic binder. They are especially worn by Asante kings and regarded as the beads of a great or wealthy man. The Akosu, similarly large, but without a dark core, is one of the beads of the Ewe kings. These beads are rare and expensive; the presence of gold flakes in the body or the core may be diagnostic of genuine Bodom and Akosu.

Kiffa beads are made by women in Mauritania in and around the town of Kiffa. A core is formed (or a European bead used) and colored glass laboriously poured on for decorations, often quite rich and sometimes imitating European beads. The larger round bead was not fused quite correctly.

Two valuable old powder-glass beads are the Bodom (the biconical one) and the Akosu (the barrel shaped one). Bodom have dark cores and are the beads of the Kings of Asante. Akosu do not have dark cores, and are beads of the Ewe Kings. Both specimens have traces of gold flakes; the Bodom in the core and the Akosu on the surface.

Although powder-glass beads are not highly regarded by most Western collectors, this attitude will surely change as the different types come to be recognized and the antiquity and traditions of the process become better known. This has already happened to Kiffa beads and Bodom, and will catch up with others as well.

Bida Glass Beadmaking

The only traditional glass beadmaking south of the Sahara which does not use the powder-glass technique is located in Bida, Nigeria. The beadmakers have been plying their craft there for centuries, but their origins and the origins of their glassmaking are mysteries.

The older glass beads from Bida are very dark green or brown in color, and decorated only sparingly. The glass itself was made locally with sand containing considerable iron, producing the dark colors. Although this glass has occasionally been made since the 1930s, it is hardly ever used now. The raw material these days are broken bottles and other forms of scrap glass.

The beadmakers melt a piece of the bottle over their fire and allow it to drip onto an iron rod (which leaves a black perforation deposit) to form a bead. The colors are limited to usual bottle colors — blue, green, amber, etc. The designs are limited, too, but the workers have the ability to expand their styles any time in the future.

Metal Beadmaking

Africa is a treasure house of raw materials, including precious and base metals. By the eighth century West Africans had learned to make ornaments and other objects by the lost-wax technique. This seems to have been first used in Nigeria and passed from there to people living to their west. The method involves sculpting or building a form in wax which is covered with successive layers of clay to make a mold. Molten metal is poured in through a hole left for the purpose, melting the wax so it runs out that or another hole. After the metal sets, the mold is broken and the piece removed, filed smooth, cleaned and polished.

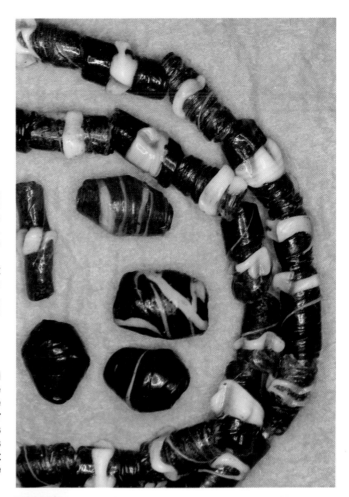

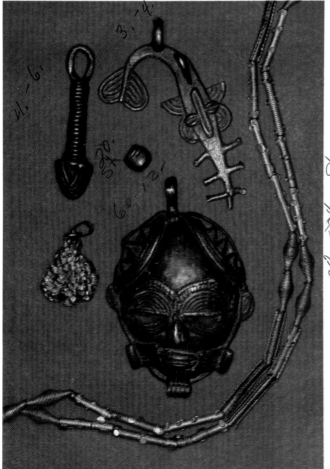

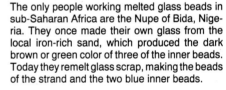

The only people working melted glass beads in sub-Saharan Africa are the Nupe of Bida, Nigeria. They once made their own glass from the local iron-rich sand, which produced the dark brown or green color of three of the inner beads. Today they remelt glass scrap, making the beads of the strand and the two blue inner beads.

Lost wax brass casting is practiced by several African groups. The strand of beads, the mask pendant and the mudskipper pendant were made by the Baoule of the Ivory Coast. The phallus and worn bead are Kirdi from Cameroon. The gold nugget pendant is from Senegal.

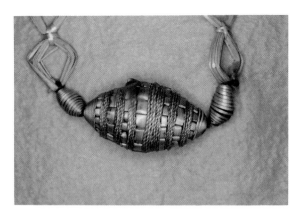

Even better than cast brass is cast gold, but not every one can afford it. This bead is made of wax intricately covered with straw in imitation of valued gold beads from Mali.

The practitioners of this technique used gold where it was available, especially in Ghana (the old Gold Coast), the Ivory Coast and Senegal. They more commonly use bronze or brass in these countries, with some forms in these metals duplicating the gold beads. Smiths in Nigeria and the Kirdi of Cameroons are two other well-known workers in brass. In Mali wax forms are covered with straw to duplicate the filigree gold beads which are out of the price range of ordinary women.

Silver is also favored by some African groups, as widely separated as the highlands of Ethiopia and the Tuareg nomads of the central savanna and Sahara. Ironically, the major form among both groups is the cross. The Ethiopians value crosses because many of them are Christians. These crosses and much of their other jewelry are made by itinerant smiths. The Tuareg wear what is called "the cross of Agadez," probably unrelated to any Christian symbolism. The Tuareg do not make their jewelry, rather the Inadan, a people generally subservient to, but not slaves of, the noble Tuareg, do the work. The Tuareg rely on them not only for jewelry and crafts, but many other services. The cross of Agadez has connections with other jewelry forms, such as the *talhakimt*, a pendant traditionally made of carnelian or other stones and perhaps ultimately imported in centuries past from India.

Stone Beads

The use of stones for beadmaking is very old in Africa. Wherever there were interesting or colorful stones, they were exploited as soon as there were techniques to shape and bore them. In the Sahara, beads of green amazonite, mottled black and white granite/dolomite, quartz and agate date back centuries. Additionally, many stone beads on the African market, including carnelians and agates, are imports; some of them were specifically made by the Indian industry for export to the continent.

Ilorin, Nigeria, was home to the remnant of an old stone beadmaking industry that traces its beginnings back to Old Oyo, the ancient capital of the Yoruba people. The primary stone worked was red jasper, though carnelians and agates were sometimes used as well. The tubular or barrel shaped beads are called *lantana* and are highly valued. The production process was laborious, as the holes were pecked out with tiny tools hammered at the ends; the apertures of the perforations show this operation. It took a man a day to make only a couple of beads. Production ended in the 1930s and has not been nor is likely to be revived.

Silver pendants made in the shapes of crosses. The two on top are made by the Inadan for the Tuareg. The two on the bottom are made in Ethiopia, a Christian country.

Stone beads typically found in African collections. Top center is a prehistoric locally made quartz bead; note the pecked perforation. To its right is a small amazonite bead, greatly desired in prehistoric times. To its left is a carnelian bead from the medieval period. The long red bead in the center is a Lantana bead made in Oyo or Illorin, Nigeria. The three carnelian beads (large bicone, "date" bead and diamond tabular) are old imports from India. The white agate bead is also from India, as is probably the ring-and-triangle shaped Talhakimt. The green bead on the bottom is malachite from Zaire.

Another red stone bead is made by the Krobo in Ghana. It is called *abo* and the material from which it is made is bauxite. This aluminum ore is important to the economy of Ghana, since the world's largest man-made lake, Lake Volta, was built to provide electricity for smelting bauxite. The Abo bead industry, which may go back a century or more, tries to remain as secretive as possible.

Shell Beads

Shells are worn all over the continent, and many have important historical links with local cultures. Cowrie shells have been used for money as well as decoration in Africa for a long time, just as they have in Asia. In some parts of the continent, such as Angola, they were gathered locally and traded inland for this purpose. In other areas, such as West Africa, they were introduced early by traders, including Arabs. They are still commonly found decorating all sorts of items.

Conus shells took on special importance in several areas. They were introduced by Arab slave traders, and became valuable currency. In East Africa they became important status symbols, worn as whole discs or discs cut in half. In the 1870s the British destroyed as many of them as they could find in British East Africa, because of their presumed links to paganism. When crime greatly increased due to the lack of currency, they had porcelain copies of the shells made in Bohemia with serial numbers on them. In time, the Bohemians took the design and made glass copies, some of which barely resemble Conus shells at all. In West Africa, too, Conus shells are well liked. Mauritanian women wear carved ones in their hair, along with locally made stone imitations.

In southern Africa ostrich egg shell beads are still being made. The !Kung San of the Kalahari desert, who produce them, have formed a cooperative in Botswana which assures that the lion's share of the price of these beads go to the makers and not middle men and dealers. In addition, the shell of the giant African land snail is large enough to make disc beads by the heishi technique (grinding a string of disc blanks together), and these are also popular on the market.

One last shell should be mentioned because it has caused considerable confusion. Large rectangular beads perforated lengthwise are known as "hippo teeth." They have nothing to do with the river horse, however. They were cut from the giant Arca clam and are becoming increasingly scarce. A few beads of other shapes are also made from Arca shell. They all have Czech glass imitations.

Abo is the Krobo name for beads they make from bauxite. An aluminum ore, the source of the bead material is not far from the sources for industrial production, powered by the Akosombo Dam, which has created Lake Volta in Ghana, the world's largest man-made lake.

Some organic beads from Africa. The ostrich eggshell is identified by its pitted dots. The large disc is from the giant African land snail. The bones are fish vertebrae.

After the British destroyed valued Conus-shell-top disc beads in East Africa, they were forced to replace them with something similar. Eventually the design became standard for the ever-imitative Czechs. These glass beads resemble Conus shell tops cut in half. *Courtesy Rita Okrent.*

Large Arca shells are cut into flat rectangular beads in Africa. They are known as "hippo teeth," which has befuddled many a writer. Czech glass imitations were also made.

Beadwork, Gris-gris and other Beads

Beadwork is popular in much of Africa, and is of special importance to many societies. Whether it be the stand-out collars of the Maasai, the complex work done as a royal monopoly in Camaroons, Zulu love letters, the outstanding work of the Ndebele or the loving covering of wooden idols with strings of beads, it is a peculiarly expressive and decorative form.

Many of the larger and more notable pieces are either not for sale or have been bought by museums and other major collections. What is most available on the market today are items made for export. However, this does not diminish the work put into them or the beauty of the objects.

Gris-gris, an old term of uncertain origin, is used all over West Africa to refer to a charm. Initially it was a small leather case into which a magical formula was sewn and worn for protection. Old ones can still be found, but most on the market now are simply leather pieces with cowries or other beads sewn on them.

The list of African beads is enormous, and we cannot cover all of them here. Many local materials are employed, and others are reworked. Tiny clay beads are made in Mali and were sold a few years ago as having been looted from archaeological sites. In Kenya cattle bones are cut and shaped, and plugs put in them to make the holes a usable size; some of them are further decorated with a process that puts dark patterns on them. Many seeds, roots and leaves are used for beads, sometimes as amulets or for medicinal purposes and sometimes for decoration. In Ghana, young men make beads from bamboo stems and give them to their girlfriends.

The recycling of materials is also common. Almost any outside object that works has been strung as a bead by someone. In Nigeria the thick bases of glass bottles are ground into beads and drilled. Aluminum beads are made by grinding bolts into round forms. Plastic objects are melted and made into beads. The large powder-glass bead industry is by no means the only one involved in reclaiming castoffs of the modern world to make into an attractive ornament.

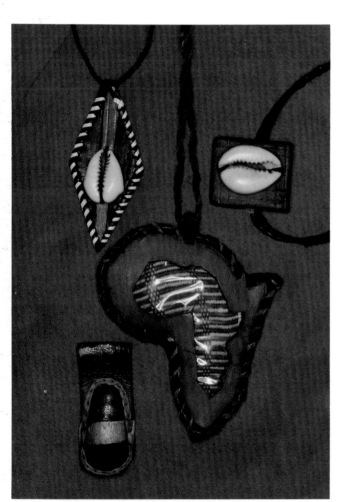

A gris-gris is a small pouch which carries a piece of magical writing. They are still considered effective, but similar pouches without writings are also sold. The tricolored one with the cowrie and small one at bottom are from the Ivory Coast; the bracelet with the cowrie is from Mali. The idea has been expanded with the attractive African pendant lined inside with Kente cloth from Ghana.

Cattle bone is bleached, polished and often colored by a batik-like process in Kenya. The craft appears to be rather new, and new designs are coming on the market.

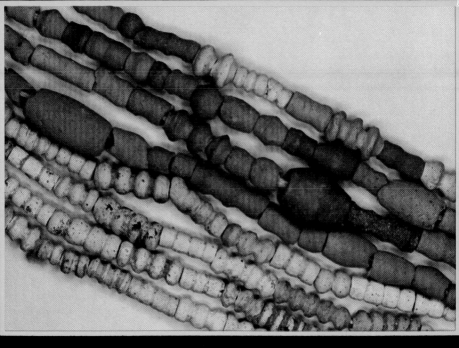

Small clay beads from Mali. These were originally sold as ancient beads dug up from around the old trading center of Jenné. They are, however, now so common and cheap that no one believes this anymore.

Nigeria, the largest African country, makes many sorts of beads. The large red powder-glass beads are no longer being produced. The other beads were ground from bottles and drilled. When they

Two large beads (more than one inch, 3 cm long) made by modern American beadmakers. The black and white bead-in-a-bead was made by Stephan Powers; the blue and white horned eye bead by Patricia Frantz.

Americans have had a long love affair with home-made beads. The papier-mâché bead at top right and cloth bead at top right are by Sue Brown of Dallas, TX. The rolled paper beads were popular in the early 20th century. The two sealing wax beads were made by the author.

Although the Americas were populated from Asia tens of thousands of years ago, climatic changes at the end of the Ice Ages closed the corridor between the two halves of the world. Afterwards, the Western Hemisphere developed independently of the Eastern, and the two regions did not know about each other's existence. All that changed beginning on October 12, 1492. Since then the world has never been the same and the bead story has had several exciting new chapters added to it.

THE BACKGROUND

Natural materials, first locally gathered and then traded greater and greater distances, were used for the earliest beads in America. Several thousand years B.C. shell beads were an important trade item from both the Atlantic and Pacific coasts to the interior regions, where they were not available. Catlinite or pipestone, an indurated clay found in Minnesota, was quarried and shipped all over North America to be used for smoking pipes and beads.

In Mexico, Central America and parts of South America sophisticated civilizations developed which could marshal resources from far and wide and support the luxurious life styles associated with their Emperors. Turquoise from the American southwest, red thorny oyster shells from the Pacific, pearls from the Caribbean and Pacific, gold and silver from deposits in Mexico, amber from southern Mexico and above all, jade from Costa Rica and Guatemala were used by the kings and nobles of the Olmec, Maya, Zapotec, Mixtec and Aztec cultures.

In South America the Incas did the same thing. From the coast came shiny oyster shells, cut to reveal their mother of pearl, and the red thorny oyster. Gold and silver were used in abundance, and all valuable materials were concentrated in the hands of the Inca himself. Other parts of South America also valued stones and gold. The Tairona culture of Columbia excelled in cutting beads from hard stones. Sodalite from Chile was traded widely. Gold, gold alloys and even platinum were used for spectacular ornaments.

The coming of the Europeans upset the entire picture. The newcomers already valued some beads and bead materials in use in the Americas. They thought nothing of killing to gain gold or silver and enslaving thousands of people to work the mines. American pearls were the biggest ever seen, and soon natives were forced to dive for them; in a few decades the pearl beds were exhausted. Jade was new to the Europeans, but when the Spanish heard that it was good for the colic, every piece they could find was sent back to Spain, ground up and drunk. Virtually nothing remains of the American treasures the Spanish encountered.

The Europeans changed the use of beads in many ways. In the case of wampum, discussed in Chapter Three, sacred tubular shell beads were transformed into currency for the settlers. Part time wampum production by Native Americans did not meet the new demand, and manufacturing was taken over by white-run factories, the last of which closed only at the end of the 1800s.

The other major change the Europeans made was bringing in new beads, especially European glass beads. On his first voyage alone, Columbus carried at least two sorts of glass beads, one apparently chevrons, as well as beads of amber and carnelian. Glass beads soon became standard trade items, even approaching currency in many dealings between the new settlers and the original inhabitants. They had to be the right beads. Explorers Lewis and Clark, for example in the early 1800s, found that they had not brought the proper beads to the Columbia basin and almost starved as a result.

5.00 - 10.00
st-

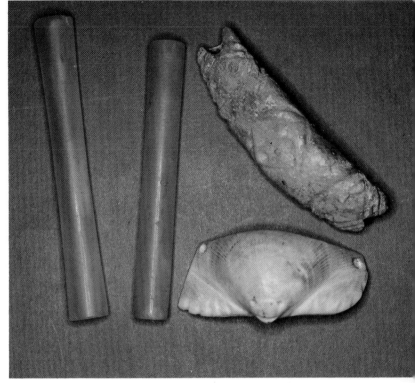

Precolumbian beads from Central and South America. The long stone beads were made by the Tairona of Columbia. The large orange colored Spondylus shell bead is from Peru. The shell pendant shaped like a bat is from Costa Rica. *Courtesy Joyce Griffiths.*

The West has long captured the American imagination. These strands were likely made in imitation of Native American work. The shell bird "fetishes" are Zuni. The "liquid silver" consists of long thin silver tubes.

GLASS TRADE BEADS IN NORTH AMERICA

The glass trade beads which came into the present territory of the United States and Canada reflected many different forces. One was local demand; if a bead was not "current," it would not be any good for trade. Another was the decision of the trader; all too often their attitudes were to foist off the shabbiest possible products to their customers that they could get away with. A third was the availability of the beads themselves; most glass beads were the types we have met when discussing Europe and China. We shall here look at their patterns of trade.

Very early in the trade the Spanish carried a pair of beads with them, which have become markers for their presence. One was the old seven layered chevron, often of small size. The other was a long square drawn tube with a dark core covered with a layer of white and then blue; the tubes are sometimes twisted. These are called "Nueva Cadiz beads" after the archaeological site in Venezuela where excavators first identified them. We find these two beads together in Florida, Texas, Peru, Mexico and across the Pacific in the Philippines.

The bulk of the early glass beads brought into the New World from the 1500s to the 1700s were Venetian drawn beads. In addition to chevrons and the Nueva Cadiz beads (we are not sure who made them), the common beads on early sites along the Atlantic were green hearts with an opaque red coat over a translucent green center, a peculiarly striated "early blue," "gooseberry" beads with white stripes on a clear base, and "flush eyes" which were rounded drawn beads decorated with a few fancy mosaic chips.

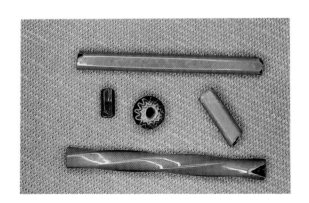

Beads typically brought by the Spaniards on their explorations. The multilayered, squared blue beads are called Nueva Cadiz after the archaeological site where they were first found; some are twisted. The seven layer chevron is typical of trade as well. These beads are known together in Texas, Florida, Mexico, Venezuela, Peru and the Philippines.

Beads of the early European trade into North America resemble those traded to West Africa at the same time. All are apparently Venetian and all but the two small beads at upper right (barleycorn beads) and the gray bead below them are drawn. The red tubes have green cores. The large blue bead at bottom is called an "Early Blue" by some archaeologists. The white bead in the center was further decorated with a mosaic chip and is called a "Flush Eye" bead. Note the multiple layers on the small beads.

There were also some wound beads in the early trade. A small one popular for a long time was called "barleycorn" by traders. It was usually white or black and resembles the grain for which it is named. Venetian and Dutch wound beads found favor later.

On the West Coast, the Spanish and later the Russians were importing beads from China. These were mostly simple wound beads, the most important one being light blue in color. It came to be called the "Chief bead" in the northwest and the "Padre bead" in the southwest. Other Chinese beads are found in heirloom collections in remote Mexican villages.

By the 1800s new sorts of beads were being brought into the trade, largely because Europe was producing different styles. Bohemia was now a major player and Venice was making a larger number of lamp-wound beads. Some of these beads appealed mostly to the white community, while others were popular with Native Americans.

The cornerless hexagonals of Bohemia were called "cut beads" in the trade and were popular from about 1830 to 1900. Venetian lamp wound beads were relatively expensive and appealed especially to the Crow and Blackfoot in the northwest. Beadwork, possibly first introduced through European examples, became very fashionable with native Americans. It soon replaced the visually similar quillwork and became an integral part of their ornamental repertoire.

Into the twentieth century beads continue to be imported into North America and are being worn, sewn and used in many ways. The idea of "costume jewelry" has now became firmly entrenched and respected. Not all costume jewelry consists of beads, but beads play an important role in the designs.

Every decade or so there are changes in bead styles. For example, before World War I long ropes of pearls and jet (both often imitation) were favored. In the 1920s even longer strands of colored glass came into vogue. The 1930s saw shorter chains and chokers of glass beads, with much attraction for plastic beads, some of them as expensive as a good dress.

During World War II there was little costume jewelry, while after the war crystal and jet rebounded. By the 1950s multiple strands of German and Japanese beads in both plastic and glass were in vogue, and the Austrian *aurora borealis* became an instant hit. Early in the 1960s was a trend toward smaller beads, but then the "hippy" era brought beads, including old trade beads now being exported from Africa, to the fore for both men and women. This and the growing sophistication of ethnic jewelry on one hand and fine costume jewelry on the other have all contributed to bead wearing since.

CONTEMPORARY ART BEADS

An exciting new phase of bead collecting has developed in the United States in the last few years: beads produced by ceramic and glass masters. As beads have become more popular, an increasing number of craftspeople have been making them, including some of the most interesting beads made anywhere.

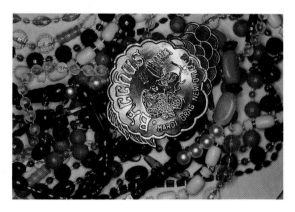

Americans even play with their beads. These plastic beads (replacing earlier glass ones) were thrown out from floats to the celebrating crowd in New Orleans' Mardi Gras parade in 1988.

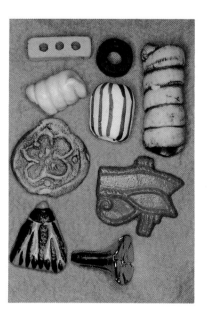

In the 1960s and 1970s clay beads were made for a large audience interested in Earth tones and beads which could be used for macramé. Many of the producers are now out of business. Two at upper left are by Earthworks, the one at upper right is by Earthly Endeavors, the two in row two are by Unos, left one in third row by Amesbury. The other three beads are faience made by Carol Strick.

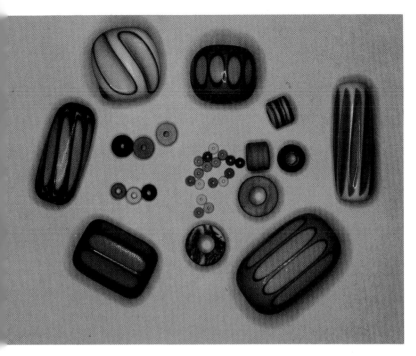

One of the survivors of the clay bead craze was Howard Newcomb, who works in porcelain. The smaller beads are quite regular and made by machine. The chevrons are a new line and a tour-de-force.

One branch works in clay. Its history began in the late 1960s and early 1970s when there was a demand for simple beads in earth tones and large beads with large holes to be incorporated into macramé work. Beadmaking units of varying size were founded to meet these demands. Few survive, but those few make some spectacular products.

One is Howard Newcomb of Portland, Oregon, who has invented and built a machine for producing fine "seed bead" sized porcelain beads which he combines into intricate jewelry pieces. His experimenting has led him recently to make the world's first porcelain chevron beads, of special interest to many collectors. Another is Joyce Whittikar, formerly of Los Angeles, now of Cambridge, Massachusetts. Her beautiful porcelain creations have a very organic atmosphere about them, incorporating human, floral and other motifs. The beads are made for specific pieces which she imaginatively constructs. Many are further incised with lines of poetry.

Another branch works in glass. The studio glass movement which developed by the inventions and processes pioneered by Dominick Labino and Harvey Littleton has become a major creative force in many parts of the country. Beadmaking is an important offshoot of this craft.

Another survivor of the clay bead fad is Joyce Whitiker, who also works in porcelain. Her elaborate beads can take up to a day to make. Many are inscribed with verses. The mask pendant was in the Mask Exhibit at the 1976 Olympics. The shawl lady is more recent.

Modern American beadmakers are increasingly turning toward glass. Some work in drawn glass, with each bead individually finished. The long bead in the center and those above are by Dudley Giberson. The next row is by Tom André, and the last row by Sara Young.

The work of Joyce Whitiaker in the early 1990s has moved to a new pallet of colors and the use of gold outlining her designs.

A leader in the glass beadmaking movement in the U.S. is Brian Kerkvliet. This bead was made to commemorate the 1990 Bead Conference in Washington. In addition to the mosaic face, it has a ying-yang symbol and a dZi bead, the symbol of the conference.

Matching the supreme challenge of drawn beads are the chevrons made by Art Seymour. The blue one at lower left has 11 layers. The others are all unusual in different ways.

Lamp-wound beads in the U.S. are getting increasingly complex. Down the left side and at the bottom are beads by Frantz Art Glass. The sunburst at top is by Sacred Eye. The blue bead and the pitcher next to it are by Salamander Selections. The two beads at right, row three, are by Tom Holland.

Among beadmakers who draw glass beads, two were established in the 1970s. One is Tom André of Clear Lake, Washington, who was once a partner with David Stone in the Tomato Tree Studio, also a beadmaking concern. The other is Dudley Giberson of Warner, New Hampshire, whose complex beads are made with machines he has invented. More recently Art Seymour of Doyle, California has been making glass chevron beads of considerable complexity and sometimes size; some have up to 15 layers.

Many commercial wound glass beadmakers are clustered in Washington state and belong to the Ring of Fire Bead Guild. Brian Kerkvliet (Gossamer Glass, Bellingham, WA) has taught several others in the guild. His speciality are fancy picture canes incorporated into beads. Sage Powers (Sage Beads, Bellingham), Patricia and Michael Franz (Franz Art Glass, Sheldon, WA) and Julie Clinton and Will Stokes (Blue Flame Studios, Bellingham) are other members who have been doing increasingly intricate lamp-wound beads. New glass beadmakers are springing up all the time, producing unusual and highly collectible products. Tom Holland of Mt. View, Arkansas, for example, entirely self-taught, was inspired by old trade beads, and is now an up-and-coming beadmaker.

Faience is the medium of Carol Strick of Hobe Sound, FL. She intensely studied the history of this once lost art, visiting faience centers of the Middle East and collecting samples of raw material for experiments. Once she perfected her craft, she became well-known for replications of ancient faience jewelry, much of it sold through museum shops.

BEADS IN MEXICO

The bead story does not stop at the Rio Grande. Before contact with Europe, the southern part of the Western hemisphere had the most interesting beads. Research into beads in Central and South America has yet to be carried out, but it appears that what happened in Mexico is typical of the rest of Latin America.

The wondrous beads made in ancient Mexico and Central America were hardly appreciated by the Spaniards looking for treasure. Every bit of gold or silver they could find was melted down into ingots and every jade bead ground up and swallowed as medicine. The other beads were ignored.

The Spanish imported their strict medieval guild system to the Americas from the beginning. There was a silversmith with Cortez when he conquered the Aztecs, and he was soon joined by many others. The

Taxco, Mexico, was historically rich in silver, and has revived a silver working tradition in the last fifty years. The earring at the bottom with abalone shell is from the 1950s; the other pieces are more recent. Round beads are made by shaping two halves in a dop and fusing them; note the half beads from the Los Castillos shop.

activities of the guild were tightly controlled by the crown, which extracted its annual fifth of the production. Spanish jewelers flocked to the new lands and immediately took over operations. Native jewelers, just as talented, were relegated to menial jobs and could never become masters or guild officers.

In every sphere of artistic life, Spanish practices and tastes dominated. Only with mundane utilitarian objects such as pottery were the local people left to their own crafts. Beads were not important to the Spanish except for pearls and coral necklaces and rosaries. Beads for the native people were imported from China.

After the Revolution of 1910, the guild system began to collapse. Eventually, people took advantage of the freedom to do whatever they liked, and some chose to make beads. In modern Mexico there are a number of bead industries. Black polished clay beads are made in San Bartolo Coyotepec near Oaxaca, pink sun-fired clay beads in villages around Iguala and brightly glazed beads near San Miguel de Allende. Silver beads and other ornaments are made at Taxco, where there are also some stone beadworkers, though most work around Iguala. Veracruz has bead industries in shell, black coral and tortoise shell. Glass beads are produced in Guadalajara. At Puebla and Tehuacan beads are made from banded alabaster, wrongly called onyx. And in the village of Simojovel, amber beads are produced.

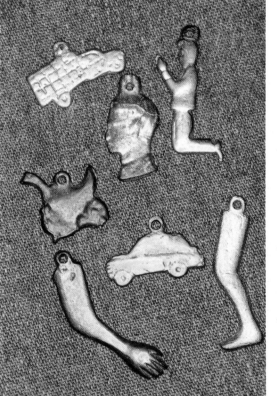

The Roman Catholic religion was securely established in Latin America, and along with it the devotion of depositing small effigies of sick parts of the body or objects wished for at holy places. Milagros are popular in Mexico and widely used for jewelry in the U.S. *Courtesy Naomi Rubin.*

Mexicans have become masters at making hard stone beads, work centered in Iguala and Taxco. This group includes rock crystal, black obsidian, blue sodalite, green aventurine and brown and yellow tiger's eye. The large bicone in the center and the melon shaped bead are serpentine. The two clear beads on the bottom are not, as they appear, prehistoric rock crystal but modern imitations made of glass.

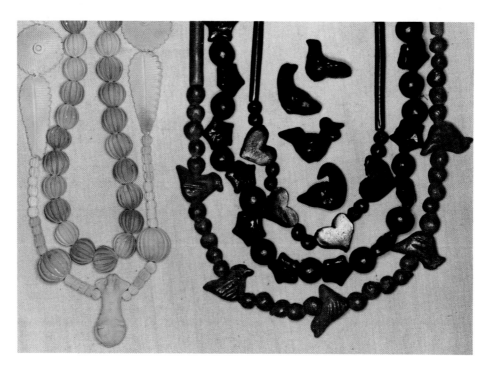

Clay beads from Mexico. On the left are sun-baked strands made in Mayatepec near Iguala. The beads on the right are from San Bartolo Coyotepec near Oaxaca. There the gray clay fires to a red unless it is burnished and given a special smoke treatment at the end of the firing, which turns it black.

But, when visiting these industries, one thing strikes the interviewer. They are all new. Beads are made not by traditional methods, but with machines and techniques invented by the present operator or a parent. The black clay of Oaxaca was developed only in 1952. The silver industry in Taxco was moribund until enlivened by Americans and dedicated Mexicans in the 1930s. Only the amber industry can be traced historically through the centuries, and it alone is using methods that echo pre-contact procedures.

These bead industries were not born until the restrictions against employment and the long-outdated imported guild system were abolished. There was a demand for beads, and individuals struck out on their own to fulfill the need, using materials at hand and any techniques they could devise. Only the amber industry survived because it is located in the Lacandon jungle and was not worth the Spaniards conquering. Knives, sandpaper and sharpened bicycle spokes have replaced stone blades, stone grinders and sharp thorns as tools in this industry that survived centuries of cultural destruction.

The variety of beads being made in Mexico changes yearly. At left is a strand of steatite beads from Iguala. The blue beads are of onyx marble. The beads in the center are black coral from Veracruz. The shell beads are also made at Veracruz, the small ones being imported from Italy.

THE REST OF LATIN AMERICA

Although no thorough research has been done on beads south of Mexico, some highlights of current production can be mentioned.

Dominica, (the Dominican Republic) has come to rival the Baltic area as a producer of amber. The large deposits are open to citizens and substantial quantities are being mined. Dominican amber tends to be light in color and is sometimes treated to darken it. It contains a much higher proportion of fossils than does Baltic amber, and interesting studies have been done lately, as frogs, mushrooms and other creatures have been identified; ancient DNA has even been extracted. Dominica also produces a bead made of a blue stone with red spots under the trade name "Larimar", which is actually a fairly scarce mineral named pectolite.

Peru produces a line of beads popular because they are colorful, attractive and not expensive. They are made from clay treated in the traditional manner, then formed into beads and painted, principally in the village of Pisac. Some are lacquered, while others are glazed. These fun beads have improved greatly in style and sophistication in only the last few decades, often thanks to the help of American exporters.

There are few glass beadmakers in Latin America. Arte Murano, outside Caracas, Venezuela, is a colony of immigrants from Venice. They used to make millefiori beads, but the master who did that work has passed away and no one has replaced him.

There are many, many other beads made in Latin America, including those of seeds, clay, shell and stone. Few have yet penetrated the world market, but who knows where they will be tomorrow?

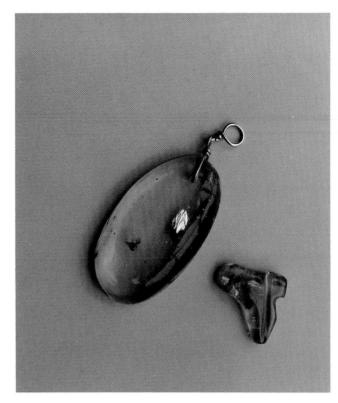

Mexican and Dominican amber are not as well known as Baltic amber, but have some special characteristics. Note the insects in the large Dominican pendant, which contains six, and in the boot from Simojovel, Mexico.

The colors of Amber from Simojovel, Mexico. The yellow is most common, but orange and a deep "cherry" red are also found.

From Peru come brightly painted beads made from the local clay. Over time, they have evolved in style and finish. The four to the upper left of the center bead were made in the 1970s. The five to its upper right are varnished. The center bead and the ones below it have been glazed.

50. .60
5t

3.00 - 10.00

16. 20

.8 .12

125. 5t. 18.

140. 5t.

45 - .80

Don't be taken in by fancy names for common beads. The two glass and two carnelian beads on the top have been called Roman, but the glass ones are 19th century and the carnelian ones no more than 18th century. The large blue and green beads are called "Nueva Cadiz," but are 350 to 400 years newer than true ones. The cornerless hexagonal at left is often called "Russian," but is not. The wound blue annular and barrel beads are called "Dogon" and "Dutch;" both names are misleading. Also watch out for "Lewis and Clark bead," "French Ambassador bead," "Manhattan bead" and others. Good luck!

SOME BEAD FALLACIES

Because beads have been around for so long without being adequately studied, people interested in them have been left to their own devices concerning their history and what to call them. This has led to considerable confusion, which can sometimes be placed at the door of professionals and sometimes blamed on collectors. We cannot clear up all these misconceptions, but a look at a few may be instructive.

The best known one, familiar to every American and most European schoolchildren, is the claim that Manhattan Island, the heart of New York City, was bought by Peter Minuet for $24 worth of beads and other trinkets. I was recently shown a mixed group of beads, crude shell discs and some old trade beads, marked with a label saying "one of 26 strands of wampum used to buy Manhattan." They were not wampum, but could they have been used to buy Manhattan?

Not likely. We know the Dutch paid the equivalent of 60 gold guilders for rights to the island. Surely they did not pay in money but in trade goods. The deed has been lost. A few months later, Staten Island was also bought by Minuet. Though that deed is also lost, it was partly copied before it disappeared. No beads were in the list of goods. Wampum was, but only as a sign of the agreement (the Staten Island Indians made their own wampum), as were drilling awls, to make more wampum.

American historians didn't even know about the purchase until more than two centuries later when old Dutch documents were published in the 1840s. The first few historians to make use of these documents mention no beads, but a history of New York City published in 1877 boldly asserted, "[Minuet] then called together some of the principal Indian chiefs, and offered beads, buttons and other trinkets in exchange for their real estate. They accepted the terms with unfeigned delight, and the bargain was closed at once." Martha J. Lamb was taking literary licence, but nearly every historian since has adopted her story literally.

Beads may have been used, but there is no proof for it.

Not only is the story wrong, but so was the ascription of the beads I was shown. How could this happen? Many popular collectible beads have had stories attached to them. They are romantic and fun, and the beads come to be known through them. But, most of these stories are just fun.

The bead known as a "Lewis and Clark" had nothing to do with either man. Beads like this were made decades after their famous exploration of the Louisiana Purchase. Besides, we know what sorts of beads Lewis and Clark took with them, and none resemble these fancy Venetian lampwound beads.

The name "Russian bead" or "Russian blues" is commonly attached to the cornerless hexagonals of Bohemia. It is a term Alaskan collectors coined, and though it is evocative, it is misdirected. Not only were they not Russian productions, but the Russians hardly handled them. When the Russians were furnishing their own beads for the Alaskan trade they got them from Europe and Asia, but this was before these beads were produced, and they are not found on early Russian contact sites. They came into the Alaskan trade much later and were supplied by Americans and the British.

I am not sure where the "French Ambassador Bead" really got its name, but I have heard so many conflicting and unbelievable stories that I am sure it is also misnamed. So are many beads being imported from Africa, such as "Dogon" "Aggrey" or "Roman." Nor is this only an American problem. It is more prevalent here, but is found everywhere.

Fortunately, now with increased serious work done on beads we do not have to rely on these old tales. After all, truth is much more interesting than fiction.

Finding Beads

Because of the fluid nature of the bead business and the large number of outlets, no listing of bead stores is attempted here. To check for those in your area, look under "beads" and "antique jewelry" in the Yellow Pages. For mail order and other out-of-town stores, the advertisements in *Ornament*, the listings in *The Bead Directory* (Benmour 1992) and the "Bead Board" section in the October issues of *Lapidary Journal* (beginning in 1992) will give you an excellent start.

Working with Beads

There are many publications on how to string beads and do beadwork. Bead societies and bead shops often carry such books and/or offer classes or workshops on particular projects. *The Bead Business* (in several editions) by Penny Diamanti outlines the basics of starting your own commercial venture in beads. Her shops carry one of the largest selections of books on bead subjects (Beadazzled, 1522 Connecticut Ave., Washington D.C., 20036; Beadazzled 421 N. Charles Street, Baltimore, MD 21201). Other good sources for bead books are the Bead Museum (see Seeing Beads) and the Center for the Study of Beadwork (see Institutions).

Publications

Ongoing publications concerned with beads include *Ornament*, *Lapidary Journal* and *Beads*. Newsletters of bead institutions are discussed in the next two sections. Many bead societies also have newsletters.

Ornament (formerly the *Bead Journal*) covers ancient, ethnic and contemporary jewelry, clothing and beads. It is lavishly illustrated and has long been a favorite publication of many bead people. It sells back issues as long as they are available, though they often go out of print in a few years. *Ornament* P.O. Box 2349, San Marcos, CA 92079-9806.

Beads is the journal of the Society of Bead Researchers, a professional group dedicated to serious bead studies. It is an annual with substantial articles and color plates. It can be purchased separately or obtained by joining the Society, which also brings you a semiannual newsletter. Society of Bead Researchers c/o Lester Ross, Secretary-Treasurer, P.O. Box 7304, Eugene, OR 97401.

Lapidary Journal is devoted to the hobby of rocks and minerals, including related topics, such as fossils. It is aimed at a general audience. It has been increasing its coverage of beads and now puts out an annual bead issue each October, which goes out of print very quickly. They will, however, furnish photocopies of any past articles. The April issue is a huge annual buyer's guide. *Lapidary Journal*, Circulation Department, P.O. Box 1100, Devon, PA 19333-9935.

Seeing Beads

Virtually all general museums of any size have beads, but they are not always displayed. Some, such as the Metropolitan Museum of Art in New York or the Peabody Museum at Harvard University in Cambridge MA, have large displays, while others tend to keep their beads in storage. To see these, one needs to contact the curator involved. Nonetheless, if you are a bead lover on the road a good rule of thumb is to visit any museum, because it will often pay off handsomely. Two museums are of special interest.

The Bead Museum in Prescott, AZ is exclusively devoted to beads. It has permanent and temporary displays, with shows on specific themes. It welcomes visitors year-round. You can join as a member and receive their quarterly newsletter. The Bead Museum, c/o Gabrielle Liese, 140 S. Montezuma, Prescott, AZ 86301.

The Corning Museum of Glass is a complex devoted to the display and study of glass. Much of its holdings are beads, and many are on display. For those with an interest in glass, this is a real treat. It also publishes *Journal of Glass Studies*, which often has articles of interest. Corning Museum of Glass, One Museum Way, Corning, NY 14830.

Patterning Stone Beads

No one has surpassed Beck (1934-35) on glazed beads in all these years, though these are hard to find. The literature on "etched" carnelians is extensive. For the most recent summary and bibliography see Francis (1980a). A summary of dZi beads is found in Frazier and Frazier (1992). The story of Pumtek beads is told in Francis (1993b).

CHAPTER SIX: GLASS BEADS

Background to Glass

There is an enormous amount of literature on glass. Unfortunately, most is designed for glassmakers and is rather technical or is devoted to the history of glass, concentrating on vessels and large glass objects. The *Journal of Glass Studies*, published by the Corning Museum of Glass is an excellent on-going source of specific information, as is the German periodical, *Glastechnische Berichte*, which has both technical and historical articles, many in English. For technical work Scholes and Green (1975) is a readable standard text. Weiss (1971) is a general introduction to glass history. Some recent articles of interest on glass history include Biek and Bayley (1979), Harden (1984) and Henderson (1985). Harden's bibliography is especially good.

Making Glass Beads and Decorating Them

Van der Sleen (1975) was the first to draw attention to the importance of how beads are made, though his discussion was limited. A much more detailed overview, with an excellent bibliography, though concentrating on beads in the American trade, is Sprague (1985); for a more global perspective see Francis (1983a). Strangely, there is no general work available on the how-to of making glass beads.

Glass Bead Colors

The standard and invaluable work on glass colors is Weyl (1959), though often quite technical in nature.

CHAPTER SEVEN: GLASS BEADS OF EUROPE

For all Europe, Francis (1988c) is the most complete. Since its publication important new information on the Venetian industry by Karklins and Adams (1990), Czech beadmaking by Ross and Pflanz (1989) and the French industry by Opper and Opper (1991) have appeared. Kidd (1979) also has much information. Karklins (1985a) pictures European bead sample cards from the last century. The *Margaretologist* constantly updates what is learned about European glass beadmakers.

CHAPTER EIGHT: THE MIDDLE EAST AND INDIA

The differences and similarities between glass beadmaking in the Classical World and the Islamic World have not yet been worked out; research is continuing along these lines. For the Harappan or Indus Valley Civilization the excavations reports, particularly Mackay (1938, 1943) on Mohenjo-daro and Chahnu-daro and Beck (1940) on Harappa are basic. For more recent summaries, new work and color plates see Kenoyer (1986, 1992).

For early and late Islamic Period glass beads see Francis (1989b, 1990a). For beads, jewelry and amulets especially in Egypt, the articles by Schienerl, beginning in 1978 and in many subsequent issues of *The Bead Journal* and *Ornament* are invaluable. The Qom faience industry is reported in Wulff (1966:67) and the Qorna industry in Francis (1980b).

Indian glass beads are first summarized in Francis (1982e). Many more details of Arikamedu and Papanaidupet have come to light; see Francis (1990b, 1991), the latter includes stone beadmaking. The article to call general attention to the West Indian stone bead industry was Arkell (1936); Francis (1982d) is a fuller treatment. For minor beadmaking in India see Francis (1983b). For a illustrated summary of all Indian beads see Francis (1988d).

CHAPTER NINE: THE FAR EAST

For Chinese glass beads Francis (1986b) summarizes the historical and analytical literature, while Francis (1990c) adds archaeological material and is well illustrated, though without a bibliography. For views of the current industry see Kan and Liu (1984) and Sprague and An (1990).

The story of Korean beads is found in Francis (1985b). An excellent treatment of Japanese glass, including much on beads, is Blair (1973). For Ojime see Kinsey (1991).

CHAPTER TEN: SOUTHEAST ASIA

A basic outline of beads in Southeast Asia is in Francis (1989c); the spread of the Indo-Pacific bead industry is in Francis (1991), although the Srivijayan connection had not yet been recognized. For heirloom beads see Francis (1992a). The Pumtek bead is separately discussed in Francis (1993b). Thai amulets are summarized in Francis (1985c) and Painter (1990). The Khmer metal bead industry is best covered in Dunning and Dunning (1990).

CHAPTER ELEVEN: AFRICA

In General
Beads in Africa have attracted much attention, and there is a large literature on them. *African Arts* often has articles on beads or related topics. The books by Carey (1986, 1991) cover broad regions concisely. For West Africa see Francis (1993c), with a fairly extensive bibliography. For a beautifully illustrated view of ornaments see Fisher (1984). Marie-José and Howard Opper (see Appendix) have written many articles and published several monographs on beads in West Africa.

Bead Markets and Altering Beads
For markets in Ghana and bead altering see Francis (1993c). For markets in Senegal see Steiner (1990). The altering of Hebron beads is detailed in Francis (1990a).

Powder-Glass Beadmaking
The first paper to summarize this industry is Liu (1974). The classic paper on the Krobo industry is Lamb (1976). For Kiffa beads see Opper and Opper (1989). See also Francis (1993c), with details on the Bodom and Akosu.

Bida Glass Beadmaking
This industry has often been described. Nadel (1951) and Gardi (1969) are rather complete, the latter well illustrated.

Metal Beadmaking
For lost-wax casting see Silverman (1986), Fox (1986) and Francis (1992c). For Inadan-Tuareg silver working see Kirtley and Kirtley (1979).

Stone Beads
A recent article on *lantana* beads is O'Hear (1986). The principal paper on bauxite beads is Shaw (1945).

Beadwork
Much beadwork is to be seen in Fisher (1984). Some more specific sources include: for Cameroon see Northern (1975), for the Kwazulu see Levinsohn (1980), for the Massai see Blauer (1992) and for the Yoruba see Fagg (1980).

CHAPTER TWELVE; THE AMERICAS

Background
Orchard (1975) remains a good introduction, even though originally published in 1929. A summary of beads and the bead trade derived from historical sources is Francis (1986a). Many papers in Hayes (1989) deal with shell beads in the Americas. For the southwest see Jernigan (1978). For the shell bead trade from the West Coast inland see Bennyhoff and Hughes (1987). For precious metals in pre-contact America see Bray (1978) and Jones (1985). For pre-contact jewelry see Liu (1992).

Glass Trade Beads

Karklins and Sprague (1980, 1987) are comprehensive bibliographies. Most papers in Hayes (1983) deal with this subject, with an extensive bibliography. For Dutch beads see Karklins (1985b). For the early Spanish bead trade see Smith and Good (1982). Sørensen (1971) has long been cited because of the color plates; the issue is now a collector's item, but is being reprinted in monograph form.

Contemporary Art Beads

Beadmakers in polyform are featured in Roche (1991). Contemporary bead work is the subject of Moss and Scherer (1992). For modern glass beadmakers see Bead Museum (1993). For the latest developments in these fields *Ornament* presents new artists on a continuing basis.

Mexico

The only easily obtained work in English for a background of Mexican jewelry is Davis and Pack (1963). Francis (1987b) is an issue of the *Margaretologist* devoted entirely to Mexico.

Bead Fallacies

The myth of Manhattan being bought for beads is in Francis (1986c) (reprinted by the Center). Condensed versions are in Francis (1986a, 1986d).

Rest of Latin America

For ancient beads of the Tairona in Columbia see Kessler and Kessler (1978). For ancient and modern beads of Ecuador see Kessler and Kessler (1986) for Panama see Kessler and Kessler (1988).

REFERENCES

Abbot, Robert T. 1962. *Sea Shells of the World: A Guide to the Better-Known Species*. New York: Golden Press.

Abbott, Lymon. 1871. Glass-Blowing as a Fine Art. *Harper's New Monthly Magazine* 42(249):337-54.

Allen, Jamey D. 1975-6. Amber and Its Substitutes. (3 parts) *Bead Journal* 2(3):15-20, 2(4):11-22, 3(1):20-31.

Arkell, A.J. 1936. Cambay and the Bead Trade. *Antiquity* 10(39):292-305.

Armstrong, Wayne. 1991. Beautiful Botanicals: Seeds for Jewelry. *Ornament* 15(1):66-9.

_____. 1992. Nature's Bounty. *Ornament* 16(2):66-9.

Bead Museum (1993) *The Work of Contemporary Glass Beadmakers*. Prescott AZ: Bead Museum.

Bauer, Max. 1968. *Precious Stones* (2 vols.) New York: Dover.

Beck, Horace C. 1934-35. Notes on Glazed Stones. (3 parts) *Ancient Egypt and the East* 1934(2):69-83, 1935(1):19-37.

_____. 1940. Report on Selected Beads from Harappa. Pp. 392-431 in M.S. Vats. *Excavations at Harappa*. Varanasi: Bhartiya Publishing House.

_____. 1973. *Classification and Nomenclature of Beads and Pendants*. York, PA: Liberty Cap.

Benmour, Linda (1992) *The Bead Directory* Oakland: The Bead Directory.

Bennyhoff, James A. and Richard E. Hughes. 1987. Shell Bead and Ornament Exchange Networks Between California and the Western Great Basin. *Anthropological Papers of the Museum of American History* 64(2):79-175.

Biek, Leo and Justine Bayley. 1979. Glass and other vitreous materials. *World Archaeology* 11(1):1-25.

Blair, Dorothy. 1973. *A History of Glass in Japan*. Tokyo/Corning: Kodansha/ Corning Museum of Glass.

Blauer, Ettagale. 1992. Beads that Speak. *Lapidary Journal* 46(7):20-7.

Brady, George. 1977. *Materials Handbook* (11th ed.) New York: McGraw-Hill.

Bray, Warwick. 1978. *The Gold of El Dorado*. London: Times Newspapers.

Budge, E.A. Wallis. 1968. *Amulets and Talismans*. New Hyde Park: University Books. (various editions; also published as *Amulets and Superstitions*)

Carey, Margaret. 1986. *Beads and Beadwork of East and South Africa*. Aylesbury: Shire.

_____. 1991. *Beads and Beadwork of West and Central Africa*. Aylesbury: Shire.

Casanowicz, Immanuel M. 1909. The Collection of Rosaries in the United States National Museum. *Proceedings of the United States National Museum* 36. (reprinted by the Bead Society of Northern California)

Ceci, Lynn. 1989. Tracing Wampum's Origins: Shell Bead Evidence from Archaeological Sites in Western and Coastal New York. Pp. 63-80 in Hayes (1989).

Dance, S. Peter. 1974. *The Collector's Encyclopedia of Seashells*. New York: McGraw-Hill.

Daniels, Peta. 1987. Vanity to Valour: The Complex Motivations for Personal Adornment. *Ornament* 10(4):22-7.

Davidow, Corinne and Dawes, Ginny R. 1988. *The Bakelite Jewelry Book*. New York: Abbyville Press.

Davis, Mary and Greta Pack. 1963. *Mexican Jewelry*. Austin: University of Texas.

Davis, Nancy. 1989. Conservation of Archaeological Shell Artifacts. Pp. 13-6 in Hayes (1989).

Digby, Adrian. 1978. *Maya Jades*. London: British Museum.

Dubin, Lois Sherr. 1987. *The History of Beads*. New York: Abrams.

Dunning, Duangporn and Steven Dunning. 1990. *An Ancient Khmer Beadmaking Art in Modern Thailand*. Mercer Island, WA: Hands of the Hills.

Eisenberg, Jerome M. 1981. *A Collector's Guide to Seashells of the World*. New York: Crescent Books.

Erikson, Joan Mowat. 1993. *The Universal Bead*. New York: W.W. Norton.

Fagg, William. 1980. *Yoruba Beadwork: Art of Nigeria*. New York: Rizzoli.

Farn, Alexander. 1986. *Pearls: Natural, Cultured and Imitation*. London: Butterworths.

Fisher, Angela. 1984. *Africa Adorned*. New York: Abrams.

Fox, Christine. 1986. Asante Brass Casting. *African Arts* 19(4):66-71.

Francis, Peter Jr. 1980a. Etched Beads in Iran. *Ornament* 4(3):24-8.

_____. 1980b. Beads in Egypt. *Ornament* 4(4):15-7, 49.

_____. 1982a. The Earliest Beads in India, Part I. *Ornament* 5(4):18-9.

_____. 1982b. The Earliest Beads in India, Part II. *Ornament* 6(1):14-5, 60.

_____. 1982c. *Handbook of Bead Materials*. World of Beads Monograph Series (WBMS) 5, Lapis Route, Lake Placid.

_____. 1982d. *Indian Agate Beads*. WBMS 6. Lapis Route, Lake Placid.

_____. 1982e. *The Glass Beads of India*. WBMS 7. Lapis Route, Lake Placid.

_____. 1983a. Some Thoughts on Glass Beadmaking. Pp. 193-202 in Hayes (1983).

_____. 1983b. Minor Indian Beadmakers. *Ornament* 6(3):18-21.

_____. 1984a. A Bead Potpourri. *Ornament* 7(3):29, 52-3.

_____. 1984b. Plants as Human Adornment in India. *Economic Botany* 38(2):194-209.

_____. 1985a. Abacus: Beads That Count. *Greater Washington Bead Society Newsletter* 2(2):1-3.

_____. 1985b. *A Survey of Beads in Korea*. Occasional Papers of the Center for Bead Research (OPCBR) 1. Lake Placid.

_____. 1985c. Thailand: Revolution and Ruin, Tradition and Change. *Ornament* 9(2):42-8.

_____. 1986a. *Beads and the Discovery of the New World*. OPCBR 3. Lake Placid.

_____. 1986b. *Chinese Glass Beads: A Review of the Evidence*. OPCBR 2. Lake Placid.

_____. 1986c. The Beads That Did **Not** Buy Manhattan Island. *New York History* 67(1):1-22.

_____. 1986d. Did Beads Buy Manhattan Island? *Ornament* 10(2):55-8, 73-8.

_____. 1987a. The Endangered Bead. *Ornament* 11(1):64-73.

_____. 1987b. Focus on Mexico. *Margaretologist* 1(4):1-12.

_____. 1988a. Some News About Old Beads. *Ornament* 11(4):33-4, 70-6.

_____. 1988b. When Is a Bead Not a Bead? *Ornament* 11(3):33, 66-76.

_____. 1988c. *The Glass Trade Beads of Europe: Their Manufacture, Their History and Their Identification*. WBMS 8. Lapis Route, Lake Placid.

_____. 1988d. The Beads of India. *Arts of Asia* 18(2):102-10.

_____. 1989a. *The Bead Dictionary*. WBMS 9. Lapis Route, Lake Placid.

_____. 1989b. Beads of the Early Islamic Period. *Beads* 1:21-39.

_____. 1989c. *Beads and the Bead Trade in Southeast Asia*. Contributions of the Center for Bead Research 4, Lake Placid.

_____. 1990a. Beadmaking in Islam: The African Trade and the Rise of Hebron. *Beads* 2:15-28.

_____. 1990b. Glass Beads in Asia, Part II: Indo-Pacific Beads. *Asian Perspectives* 29(1):1-23.

_____. 1990c. Glass Beads of China. *Arts of Asia* 20(5):118-27.

_____. 1991. Beadmaking in Arikamedu and Beyond. *World Archaeology* 23(1):28-43.

_____. 1992a. *Heirlooms of the Hills: Southeast Asia*. Beads and People Series 1, Lapis Route, Lake Placid.

_____. 1992b. *Handbook for the C.B.R. Bead Identification Workshop I or 20 Easy Steps to Identifying Most Beads in Most Collections*. Lapis Route, Lake Placid.

_____. 1992c. West African Perspective: Lost-Wax Brass Casting. *Ornament* 15(4):98-9.

_____. 1993a. Sumatra's Lost Kingdom. *Lapidary Journal* 47(7):108-18.

_____. 1993b. Common Intrigue. *Lapidary Journal* 47(4):41-4, 96-8.

_____. 1993c. *Where Beads Are Loved: Ghana, West Africa*. Beads and People Series 2. Lapis Route, Lake Placid.

Frazier, Si and Ann Frazier. 1992. Lines of Inquiry. *Lapidary Journal* 46(7):47-59.

Frondel, Clifford. 1962. *The System of Mineralogy (of James Dwight Dana), Volume III: Silica Minerals.* New York: John Wiley.

Gardi, René, 1969. *African Crafts and Craftsmen.* New York: Van Nostrand Reinhold.

Grigg, Richard W. and David Doubilet. 1979. Precious Corals: Hawaii's Deep-sea Jewels. *National Geographic* 155(5):719-32.

Grove, Noel and Steve Raymer. 1981. Wild Cargo: The Business of Smuggling Animals. *National Geographic* 159(3):286-315.

Hansford, S. Howard. 1950. *Chinese Jade Carving.* London and Bradford: Lund Humphries.

Harden, Donald B. 1984. Study and Research on Ancient Glass: Past and Future. *Journal of Glass Studies* 26:9-24.

Hayes, Charles F., ed. 1983. *Proceedings of the 1982 Glass Trade Bead Conference.* Research Records 16. Rochester: Rochester Museum and Science Center.

_____. 1989. *Proceedings of the 1986 Shell Bead Conference: Selected Papers.* Research Records 20. Rochester: Rochester Museum and Science Center.

Henderson, Julian. 1985. The Raw Materials of Early Glass Production. *Oxford Journal of Archaeology.* 4(3):267-91.

Jenyns, Soame. 1951. *Chinese Archaic Jades in the British Museum.* London: The British Museum.

Jernigan, E. Wesley. 1978. *Jewelry of the Prehistoric Southwest.* Santa Fe: School of American Research.

Jones, Julie. 1985. *The Art of Precolumbian Gold: The Jan Mitchell Collection.* New York: Metropolitan Museum.

Kan, Paddy and Robert. K. Liu. 1984. Chinese Glass Beadmaking. *Ornament* 8(2):38-40, 67.

Karklins, Karlis. 1985a. *Glass Beads.* Hull, Canada: Parks, Canada.

_____.1985b. Early Amsterdam Trade Beads. *Ornament* 9(2):36-41.

_____ with Carol F. Adams. 1990. Dominique Bussolin on the Glass-Bead Industry of Murano and Venice (1847). *Beads* 2:69-84.

_____ and Roderick Sprague. 1980. *A Bibliography of Glass Trade Beads in North America.* Moscow, ID: South Forks Press.

_____ and _____. 1987. *A Bibliography of Glass Trade Beads in North America: First Supplement.* Ottawa: Promontory Press.

Kelley, Lyngerda and Nancy Schiffer. 1987. *Plastic Jewelry.* West Chester, PA: Schiffer.

Kenoyer, Johnathan Mark. 1986. The Indus Bead Industry: Contributions to Bead Technology. *Ornament* 10(1):18-23.

_____. 1992. Lapis Lazuli Beadmaking in Afghanistan and Pakistan. *Ornament* 15(3):70-3, 86-7.

Kessler, Earl and Shari Kessler. 1978. Beads of the Tairona. *Bead Journal* 3(3/4):2-3, 83-5.

_____ and _____. 1986. Ecuadorian Beads: Ancient to Modern. *Ornament* 10(2):48-52.

_____ and _____. 1988. Beads of Ancient Panama. *Ornament* 11(4):20-4.

Kidd, Kenneth. 1979. *Glass Bead-Making from the Middle Ages to the Early 19th Century.* History and Archaeology 30. Hull, Canada: Parks Canada.

Kinsey, Robert O. 1991. *Ojime: Magical Jewels of Japan.* New York: Abrams.

Kirtley, Michael and Aubine Kirtley. 1979. The Inadan: Artisans of the Sahara. *National Geographic* 156(2):282-98.

Lamb, Alastair. 1976. Krobo Powder-Glass Beads. *African Arts* 9(2):32-9.

Laufer, Berthold. 1974. *Jade: A Study in Chinese Archaeology and Religion.* New York: Dover.

Levinsohn, Rhoda. 1980. Rural Kwazulu Beadwork. *Ornament* 4(4):38-42.

Liu, Robert K. 1974. Mold-made Glass African Beads. *Bead Journal* 1(2):8-14.

_____. 1975. General Considerations on the Storage and Display of Beads, With a Method for the Display of Single Beads. *Bead Journal* 1(4):17-23.

_____. 1978. Spindle Whorls: Pt. 1, Some Comments and Speculations. *Ornament* 3(3/4):87-103.

_____. 1987. India, Idar-Oberstein and Czechoslovakia: Imitators and Competitors. *Ornament* 10(4):56-61.

_____. 1992. Precolumbian Personal Adornment. *Ornament* 16(1):51-4, 83, 104.

Mackay, Ernest. 1938. *Further Excavations at Mohenjo-Daro*. Delhi: Manager of Publications.

_____. 1943. *Chahnu-daro Excavations 1935-36*. American Oriental Series 20. New Haven: American Oriental Society.

Maloney, Clarence, ed. 1976. *The Evil Eye*. New York: Columbia University Press.

Moss, Kathlyn and Alice Scherer. 1992. *The New Beadwork*. New York: Abrams.

Muller, Helen. 1980. *Jet Jewellery and Ornaments*. Aylesbury: Shire Publications.

Nadel, S.F. 1951. *A Black Byzantium: The Kingdom of Nupe in Nigeria*. London: Oxford.

Nassau, Kurt. 1984. *Gemstone Enhancement*. London: Butterworths.

Northern, Tamara. 1975. *The Sign of the Leopard: Beaded Art of the Cameroon*. Storrs, CT: University of Connecticut.

O'Hear, Ann. 1986. Ilorin Lantana Beads. *African Arts* 19(4):36-9.

Opper, Marie-José. 1990. *Scented Magic Beads in Africa*. Washington: private.

_____ and Howard Opper. 1989. *Kiffa Beads*. Washington: private.

_____ and _____. 1991. French Beadmaking: An Historical Perspective Emphasizing the 19th and 20th Centuries. *Beads* 3:47-59.

Orchard, William C. 1975. *Beads and Beadwork of the American Indians*. New York: Museum of the American Indian.

Painter, Dagmar. 1990. Sacred & Potent: The Magic of Thai Amulets. *Ornament* 13(4):36-9.

Pough, Frederick H. 1960. *A Field Guide to Rocks and Minerals*. Boston: Houghton Mifflin.

Quiggen, A.H. 1949. *A Survey of Primitive Money*. London: Methuen.

Rice, Patty C. 1980. *Amber: The Golden Gem of the Ages*. New York: Van Nostrand Reinhold.

Roche, Nan. 1991. *The New Clay: Techniques and Approaches to Jewelry Making*. Rockville, MD: Flower Valley Press.

Ross, John E. 1993. Treasured in Its Own Right, Amber is a Golden Window to the Past. *Smithsonian* 23(10):31-41.

Ross, Lester A. with Barbara Pflanz. 1989. Bohemian Glass Beadmaking: Translation and Discussion of a 1913 German Technical Article. *Beads* 1:81-94.

Safer, Jane F. and Frances M. Gil. 1982. *Spirals from the Sea: An Anthropological Look at Shells*. New York: Clarkson N. Potter.

Schienerl, Peter W. 1978. Amulet-Containers from Egypt: A Typological Study. *Bead Journal* 3(3/4):30-37.

_____. 1985. Major Trends in the Historical Development of Amulets. *Ornament* 9(2):19-25.

Schoeman, H.S. 1968. A Preliminary Report on Traditional Beadwork in the Mkhwanazi Area of the Mtunzini District, Zululand. (2 parts) *African Studies* 27(2):57-81, 27(3):109-33.

Scholes, Samuel R. and Charles H. Green. 1975. *Modern Glass Practice*. (7th ed.). New York: C.B.I.

Shaw, T.C. 1945. Bead-Making with a Bow-Drill in the Gold Coast. *Journal of the Royal Anthropological Institute of Great Britain and Ireland* 75:45-50.

Silverman, Raymond A. 1986. Bono Brass Casting. *African Arts* 19(4):60-4.

Sinkankas, John. 1965. *Mineralogy*. New York: Van Nostrand Reinhold.

van der Sleen, W.G.N. 1975. *A Handbook on Beads*. York, PA: Liberty Cap.

Slotkin, J.S. and Karl Schmitt. 1949. Studies of Wampum. *American Anthropologist* 51(2):223-36.

Smith, Marvin T. and Mary Elizabeth Good. 1982. *Early Sixteenth Century Glass Beads in the Spanish Colonial Trade*. Greenwood MS: Cottonlandia Museum.

Snyderman, George S. 1954. The Functions of Wampum. *Proceedings of the American Philosophical Society* 98(6):469-94.

_____. 1961. The Function of Wampum in Iroquois Religion. *Proceedings of the American Philosophical Society* 105(6):571-608.

Sørensen, Cloyd. 1971. The Enduring Intrigue of the Glass Trade Bead. *Arizona Highways* 47(7):10-33.

Sprague, Roderick. 1985. Glass Trade Beads: A Progress Report. *Historical Archaeology* 19:87-105.

INDEX

Captions and text are both indexed; back matter from page 121 onwards is not. Ethnic groups are designated by adding "of country" after their name: Akha of Thailand, Asante of Ghana, etc. For the U.S.A., India and Indonesia, place names are further identified by state or island.

The Author

Peter Francis, Jr.

Pete Francis, the Director of the Center for Bead Research, is internationallly known for his pioneering work. After obrtaining his Master's degree he began a life-long odyssey to visit and understand other parts of the world and its people. He lived in Europe, North Africa and the Middle East for eight years, slowly being drawn into an interest in beads.

As a collector, he soon realized that to learn about beads he would have to do the basic research himself. He studied archaeology in India and for the last fifteen years has done nothing but research beads. This work has taken him around the globe eight times and introduced him to more than a dozen languages. During this time he has worked with scores of research bodies, has visited over a hundred beadmaking industries and has searched out many remote places where beads are considered important. Always his emphasis has been on the human element of the bead story.

Francis has had hundreds of articles published around the world and has written two dozen monographs on beads. He lectures and presents bead workshops to groups as diverse as universities, museums and bead societies. He is a consultant to many institutions, including the Smithsonian. He has received a number of prizes and grants from the New York Historical Association, the Hagop Kervorkian Foundation and several bead societies. He directs the biannual Bead Expo conferences, helped establish five bead societies and has built the Center for Bead Research into a major international resource. It is no wonder that *The New York Times* has called him "the world's leading authority on beads."